John Bascom

Evolution and religion; or, Faith as a part of a complete cosmic system

John Bascom

Evolution and religion; or, Faith as a part of a complete cosmic system

ISBN/EAN: 9783337263775

Printed in Europe, USA, Canada, Australia, Japan

Cover: Foto ©Lupo / pixelio.de

More available books at **www.hansebooks.com**

EVOLUTION AND RELIGION

OR FAITH AS A PART OF A COMPLETE COSMIC SYSTEM

BY

JOHN BASCOM

Author of "Philosophy of Religion," "Natural Theology," "Words of Christ," "The New Theology"

G. P. PUTNAM'S SONS

NEW YORK
27 WEST TWENTY-THIRD STREET

LONDON
24 BEDFORD STREET, STRAND

The Knickerbocker Press

1897

PREFACE.

THE doctrine of evolution is so recent a conception, especially in its bearing on spiritual things, that we are able as yet neither to define it well within itself, nor to see its implications when taken in connection with our higher life. We do two most undesirable things: we make the notion so inflexible as to strangle our intellectual powers, and we struggle with the theory itself as something which we would gladly escape. We hope to bring some relief at both of these points; to show that evolution is not a conception in extinction of reason, nor yet a movement in overthrow of faith. Our spiritual life is involved in it and built up by it as its most comprehensive and consummate product. We in no way grasp our religious beliefs so firmly as when we see that they are woven into the entire web of events.

CONTENTS.

PART FIRST.

PAGE

EVOLUTION AS A CONCEPTION . . . 1

PART SECOND.

EVOLUTION AS GIVING UNITY TO THE FIELD OF KNOWLEDGE AND ACTION 25

PART THIRD.

EVOLUTION IN ITS PRESENT SPIRITUAL PHASES . 79

PART FOURTH.

EVOLUTION IN THE PROOFS IT OFFERS TO SPIRITUAL BELIEFS . . . 179

PART I.

EVOLUTION AS A CONCEPTION.

But still, despite the pretty perfection
    To which you carry your trick of exclusiveness,
And, taking God's word under wise protection,
    Correct its tendency to diffusiveness,
And bid one reach it over hot ploughshares,—
    Still, as I say, though you've found salvation,
If I should choose to cry, as now, "Shares!"—
    See if the best of you bars me my ration!
I prefer, if you please, for my expounder
    Of the laws of the feast, the feast's own Founder;
Mine's the same right with your poorest and sickliest,
    Supposing I don the marriage-vestment:
So, shut your mouth and open your Testament,
    And carve me my portion at your quickliest!

        ROBERT BROWNING, *Christmas-eve and Easter-day.*

PART I.

EVOLUTION AS A CONCEPTION.

NO one idea, in our generation, has accepted more change within itself, or been more productive of change in our conception of the world, taken collectively, than that of evolution. We especially need, therefore, to understand the notion in its own spiritual force, and in the modifications it has brought, and will still bring, to our religious convictions.

Evolution means different things to different persons. While it has for all some common characteristics, it is not coherently held by all as an idea whose terms are fully reconciled within themselves, and harmonized with the events of the world. It has something of that crudeness which attaches to notions that are gathering way in the public mind, but have not yet been mastered by it. The conception which it displaces is that of a physical world possessed of its own ultimate qualities, and subject, like material in the hands of a builder, to constructive processes foreign to it. The most developed form of this comparatively mechanical idea of the world has been a phase of Theism—Personal Power at work in physical things ; the two very separable from each other, and more or less repellent in their relations.

Evolution greatly alters this theory of the world. Under it the world is not so much a construction as a growth. The changes involved in its creation have been a continuous series,—gaining expression in material things, —each preparing the way for the next, and passing into it. This general movement is resolvable into minute transformations, perfectly coherent under uniform methods. Thus far there is general agreement in the conception of evolution ; but in its later unfolding, and in the relation which it is thought to sustain to previous interpreting ideas, there springs up diversity.

Evolution, as involving a close-knit series of slight changes, is one thing; evolution, in the theories it calls out of the ultimate nature of cosmic phenomena, and of the origin of the energies expressed in the movement of events, is another thing. Evolution, as a fact simply, gives a perfectly open, and an absolutely complete, field to empirical inquiry. The last subdivision of events, and their exact order of sequence, become subjects of unending investigation, and furnish us everywhere with the material of science. In no direction is this search unfruitful; in none do we put upon it any final limits.

What the rational implications of these evolutionary facts are, it is the office of philosophy to consider. The facts themselves remain the same under one theory or another of their ultimate significance. With these facts science may exclusively busy itself, raising no questions as to the rational suggestions, which, as a complete series, they may contain. There has been, however, a form of science which has added to itself a philosophical attitude, simply that it might deny the reality of any knowledge which lies beyond the phenomena themselves. The implications of the sensuous facts, one and all, seem to it vague and illusory. The mind is led to distrust one of its most universal explanatory tendencies. We believe that the best correction of this doubt is to be found in a better understanding of evolution itself.

The sensuous features and the exact order of physical facts are to be studied, whether we do or do not believe that the agents to which we have been wont to refer them are intelligible realities. The phenomenal form of organic facts is equally to be sought out, whether we accept or refuse to accept life as a plastic power. It is the office of science to give fully and accurately the sensuous facts and sequences of the world; it is the office of philosophy to render the rational ideas which are contained in these phenomena; and of religion, to disclose the spiritual affections and actions which are incident to insight. Science presents the facts of the world; philosophy interprets them in terms of reason; and religion, in terms of spiritual life. Each, in its relation to the other, is profoundly modified by the doctrine of evolution; and the truths of each are most clearly seen and enforced in connection with this conception.

Science turns from speculations that have often been hasty, vague, without authority, to a patient investigation of phenomena, the data of thought held firmly in our sensuous lives.

Its facts thus become fruitful in action and a common field of knowledge. This stability, coherence, and possible extension of inquiry have called out an enthusiasm in its behalf before unknown.

Knowledge, by virtue of the doctrine of evolution, gains certainty, universality, solidarity. Amid all the diversity of appearances, permanent constituents and fixed methods of succession are everywhere present. The web is one through the entire complexity of its pattern. We are dealing, all of us in all places and times, with phenomena which interpret each other, and are coherent with each other in one world. Our knowledge remains no variable product of diverse opinions and divided data, but becomes matter of common observation and wise rendering. This is ultimately equally true of the conclusions of science, the results of philosophy, and the convictions of religion. The difference between them lies in the slowness with which the tissue of thought spreads in succession through them. The mind thus gains release from the endless tossings of speculation, and, like one who lands with his goods on a new continent, is prepared to take possession of the field before it, and gather about it its permanent resources. This sense of certainty, arising from the abiding facts of the physical world, plants our feet on dry land after every distressful and weary voyage.

Evolution also gives a universality to knowledge quite beyond our previous experience,— a universality in time, in place, and in fulness. The stimulating power of evolution is due to the feeling it imparts of an ever-enlarging horizon. One is placed by it in the midst of all knowledge. All knowledge rises before him in full tide, and spreads itself like an ocean through all spaces. The hesitancy and stagnation of thought at any one moment are overcome by the volume of energy which everywhere envelops it. The atmosphere is kept pure and stimulating by its own dimensions.

The mind may select its directions of inquiry, and push its way backward and forward in the movement of events till the past history and future promise of the world assume with it the force of a sensible experience. Eternity ceases to be an empty word, and is filled with phenomena traceable in exhaustless sequence. Infinity, no longer a mere sound, becomes a limitless field over which the historic scroll is displayed. Nor are present sensuous facts less stimulating. Some slight clew of knowledge may be sufficient to put us in possession of a system of laws everywhere prevalent. The waves that fall vocal at our feet are dying away in murmurs that run along all shores.

While there are primary lines of power, these are so interwoven with one another as to make the web equally tenacious in whatever direction we test it. Thus if we have many successive forms of vegetable and animal life, we have also a single and a collective response of them all to their environment,—a response which renders these lives in their diversity co-ordinate with each other and with their physical conditions. These conditions, in turn, are extensively modified by these lives. So also the connections of thought, like nerves in the human body, penetrate the entire product, and leave nothing out of that great result, a comprehensible world. Equally are the highest affections fed by these tenuous fibres of knowledge,—roots in a physical soil—and become, by means of them, noble and well-nourished forms of life.

A kindred implication of evolution is the

solidarity of knowledge. Knowledge cannot be otherwise than interdependent in all its parts. The universe is wrought constructively together, and so must be our comprehension of it. The mind in its inquiries moves necessarily along the building lines that have been laid down in the growth of the world. There is no living thing and no living experience which is not genetically associated with every other living thing and living experience. As every bud in a tree may be reached from every other bud along a path of vital tissue, so there is no department of thought which may not be entered from other departments, and does not, in turn, open new ways of access to them. The mind is as much the correlative term of the universe, and the universe of the mind, as the reflections in a lake and the banks and sky about it and above it are counterparts of each other.

The slowly unfolding connections of society call out, enlarge, and instruct the ethical insight. An ever-growing tissue of moral relations transforms the world for us, leads us to a more spiritual rendering of it, makes us ever more assured of a divine element in it, and guides us to a better apprehension of that element. Thus our belief in God, the implications of that belief, and our experience of life, become one and the same vitalized product. Belief is as much an achievement as an investigation, the fastening of tendrils as the spreading of leaves, an environment as a living response to it. Belief is reaching the inner force of things and events empirically as well as weaving them together speculatively. The very word *comprehension* carries with it a double meaning,— a taking-hold of things, and an understanding of them. The two processes are inseparable. We enter on the world as a living experience. We proceed to put it together as a rational construction. Our wisdom is a higher consciousness which dawns on our lower sensuous action, and fills it with light. In this perpetual expansion of intelligence, the regnant idea is evolution,—a coherent movement universally present.

But while evolution will, with all minds, have this wide constructive force, it easily assumes two different forms, giving very diverse extension to spiritual beliefs. The notion is itself subject to that inescapable question of inner character with which we have pushed the world in all its parts, reaching a wide diversity of conclusions. We may have a mechanical evolution or a spiritual evolution, and the one or the other leaves the world in very different degrees a dead or a living thing. By a mechanical evolution we mean one in which the quality and quantity of all the agents involved are perfectly definite. The included causes are, at any moment in which we take up the process, complete. Each successive stage in the movement follows in due order, and the last is as perfectly embraced in the primary conditions as the first. This conception of evolution is unacceptable, because it assumes an extreme statement by no means involved in the facts to be explained; because we can in no way suggest the method of the successive transitions, nor render them to ourselves in terms of experience; and because it makes no provision, certainly no adequate provision, for the larger half, the spiritual half, of the world. It renders evolution in a way in which it does not embrace the entire product, but fearfully mutilates it.

By a spiritual evolution we understand one of distinct increments and of an over-ruling purpose, which in its entire process contains and expresses personal, spiritual power in the means employed, in their combination, and in their outcome. The evolution of the world is thus allied to that of a language or of an art. The physical forces are, in every stage of their development, permeated and borne forward by intellectual ones. The two terms, *physical* and *spiritual*, proceed inseparable from each other.

We accept this form of evolution because it recognizes, in their full extent and at their true value, the spiritual elements we find in the world, and which in so large a degree make up the medium in which we live and move and have our being,—the spiritual elements which alone stimulate us to the very inquiry into the world which we have in hand; because empirically the world offers to us, in living things and in their innumerable phases, what seem to be increments; because many of the modifications of life, like those which secure cross-fertilization in plants, are extensive and complicated, and cannot be divided into minute serial changes, but must be accepted as one whole; because what we term "sports" exhibit definite and extended modifications, taking place at once; because the world, taken collectively as an orderly and growing creation, calls for an explanation in clearness and force proportioned to the comprehensiveness and magnitude of this final result; and because the make-shifts of a mechanical theory, by which intellectual elements are pushed aside or minimized, are, one and all, narrow in temper, and inconsistent with evolution itself. The problem offered us in the world is at once one of single parts and of collective results. The two must glide into each other, and find interpretation together,—evolution as a series of changes, evolution as concurrent changes in one progressive whole. No theory is adequate which does not cover them both. Of the two parts of the problem, the one which makes the strongest appeal to the mind, and demands most distinctly a rational rendering, is that of the general order of the world. We cannot treat this great fact negligently, and atone for our failure by the careful way in which we have covered subordinate points. The issue of our work must be in comprehensiveness equal to the magnitude of the phenomena themselves. We may readily accept the view that the organic thing is in such immediate response to its surroundings that each change in it is the result of these joint conditions,—an action and reaction of outer and inner terms. It is on this supposition alone that the evolution of life becomes a subject of continuous and searching inquiry; but this is not equivalent to finding in these ruling circumstances absolute and sufficient causes, precisely of the same nature as the physical causes that have preceded them. The response of life to its conditions, and the transmission of the organic changes so induced, remain peculiar and inscrutable kinds of causation, and call, in the new forms they take on and in the new directions they assume, for an informing and overruling idea. The process is so disclosed to us, is so the product of correlative relations, that we may pursue it in all its manifold changes; but it never loses the character of a definitely superior, constructive movement. It is never simply a blind flow of physical forces. The physical and spiritual evolution of the world run parallel with each other, with common terms and constant interaction, but are not identical. They have each distinct lessons. The two together make the world quite as much an intellectual as a physical product.

Our thoughts, in their own unfolding,—in that evolution which is indigenous in them—

have led us universally to a recognition of three supersensuous terms on which our explanatory processes rest,—force, life, reason. Our final explanation must embrace all three. We cannot so bundle together simple forces as to make them the equivalent of life,—life, a plastic ruling power. Nor can we so extend the organic, the instinctive, and unconscious processes of life as by them to displace the activity of the reason. Evolution has issued in all of them. It is impossible that that conscious phase of being whose product science is should call out this very conception of evolution, and at the same time affirm reason to be of no significance in connection with it. Much rather does the very substance of that idea appear in this its ripest fruit.

The mechanical theory relies, in the evolution of life, on the tendency to organic changes involved in shifting, physical conditions and on natural selection, as the two productive terms by which the vegetable and animal kingdoms are built up, and built together, in the world. These causes are inadequate to the work assigned them. We plainly see that physical changes often favor and often disturb the forms of life associated with them; we do not see that these changes have any power to beget new varieties. We cannot trace any causation at this point, nor can we inductively establish any law. Varieties remain to us obscure products whose antecedents we only partially know,—antecedents which bear the appearance quite as much of occasions as of causes. We are in no way prepared to affirm that physical circumstances beget forms of life suited to themselves, nor even that the several forms of life have, as a part of their primitive endowment, the power to reshape themselves to new conditions. If we should accept this last assertion, we should be simply allowing another form of plastic power to add itself to those we already recognize as contained in the mystery of life, and are unable to include in the physical world.

If we fall back on the assertion that changing circumstances must, in living things as elsewhere, occasion new results, even if not results of a definite order, we are flung out into a boundless sea of chances, and can make no sure port. It is impossible, under simply accidental variation, to build up, by the aid of natural selection, the present order and beauty of the world. The chances are illimitable. The varieties induced would be too many, too slight, too changeable, to give any sufficient hold to natural selection. Natural selection is a constructive force that must have somewhat limited terms—terms of distinct magnitude, and that remain with it for a considerable period—if its results are to become evident. It is not a quick, heroic energy, but a slow, hesitating process. An endless flow of chances utterly disarms natural selection.

If we look directly at natural selection, all we can ascribe to it is the survival of that which is fit, not the fitness itself. The survival of that which is able to survive is no mystery: the mystery lies in the presence of life under such circumstances as to declare its power. There is no law in purely accidental variations under which fitting material for an organic kingdom would be furnished in sufficient quantity, or under which the fragments that might appear would be given any vantage-ground. There is no imperative in natural selection that anything shall survive, or that any orderly result shall be reached. The anticipatory work must be done before natural selection sets in; and for the anticipation we have provided nothing but chance.

Evolution as a Conception.

We do not care to push this line of thought further. The ground is familiar. Our purpose is simply to define that form of evolution to which we give assent. Each man, in the end, will choose between mechanical and spiritual evolution, according to his estimate respectively of physical and intellectual phenomena. As we are to be occupied, in our whole discussion, with rational relations, we cannot at the very outset overlook their distinctive characteristics, nor proceed to put our thoughts together under connections which are not themselves intellectual. A rational movement must be true to itself in resting on reasons and the coherent links of the understanding. We cannot allow reason to betray or cripple itself at the very beginning of its own explorations. In order that it may do its work, it must affirm its own powers as ultimate judge of all things.

The evolution, then, which will be involved in the present discussion, is that of a perfectly coherent unfolding of events under causes and reasons—causes which have no interest without reasons, and reasons which have no potency without causes—working together for a definite end, and accepting the transitions and increments involved in it. The web is firmly woven in every part under one pattern, but does not necessarily start with every thread or every color that may appear later. The colors rise as the design calls for them.

Force, life, reasons are the presuppositions, which attend on all our explanations of events. The thoughts of men can make nothing of the world without them. These we fully accept. The universal mind, subject to this same universal evolution, has universally reached these notions, which are the conditions of intelligent apprehension. Physical facts fall into order under the idea of force, organic facts under that of life, and intellectual ones under that of reason. They all rest with all on the same basis as essential parts of knowledge. Evolution affirms them all.

The primary and most simple of them, that of force, has not escaped as a supersensuous notion denial, yet the most fundamental law of physics is the equivalence of forces. The equality asserted does not lie between phenomena,—as the raising of one pound one foot, the burning of a certain amount of coal, the putting-forth of a given muscular effort—but between the forces which their several processes are thought to involve. All our mathematical estimates take hold by virtue of the supposition that phenomena, variable in every feature they offer to the senses, are none the less the expression of an indestructible term, *force*. It is not our purpose to try to go back of this philosophy, which lies embedded in all our experience as an evolutionary product, but under it to trace some of the later phases of intellectual life which are incident to it. We assume the rational facts of the world as our own consciousness, as language and human history, offer them to us, and confine our attention to the light which the doctrine of evolution casts upon them.

PART II.

EVOLUTION AS GIVING UNITY TO THE FIELD OF KNOWLEDGE AND ACTION.

That men with knowledge merely play'd
I told thee—hardly higher made,
Tho' scaling slow from grade to grade;

Much less this dreamer, deaf and blind,
Named man, may hope some truth to find,
That bears relation to the mind.

For every worm beneath the moon
Draws different threads, and late and soon
Spins, toiling out his own cocoon.

.   .   .   .   .   .

I know that age to age succeeds,
Blowing a noise of tongues and deeds,
A dust of systems and of creeds.

I cannot hide that some have striven,
Achieving calm, to whom was given
The joy that mixes man with Heaven:

Who, rowing hard against the stream,
Saw distant gates of Eden gleam,
And did not dream it was a dream;

But heard, by secret transport led,
Ev'n in the charnels of the dead,
The murmur of the fountain-head—

Which did accomplish their desire,
Bore and forbore, and did not tire,
Like Stephen, an unquenchèd fire.

    ALFRED TENNYSON, *The Two Voices.*

PART II.

EVOLUTION AS GIVING UNITY TO THE FIELD OF KNOWLEDGE AND ACTION.

WHAT we have already said in defining evolution has been suggestive of our present subject, the unity of knowledge and action; but the theme is so important as to call for distinct presentation.

A conception of the physical world, rapidly gaining clearness with advancing years, is that of a system of laws which completely cover its phenomena, and perfectly sustain one another. A network of law, with no flaw in its meshes, embraces the entire material world. A conception akin to this, slowly arising with it, but not yet generally accepted, is that of the unity of all fields of thought, all forms of truth. This unity is not like that of a great body of water whose tidal movements are one and the same everywhere, but like that of different seas, closely united, yet each subject to conditions somewhat its own.

A deep division between the several portions of knowledge, rendering them relatively independent of each other, has been accepted on various grounds and from various motives. The feelings which have prompted this opinion have sometimes been the satisfaction which men find in some one form of truth, and which leads them to contrast their convictions in this familiar field with assertions made in other departments, with a ready disparagement of things relatively unknown. This impression has gained ground, till knowledge has been thought by some—as by a few scientists—not to extend much beyond their own favorite subjects of inquiry. They have not seen that these fragments of truth are incapable of support except as they hold together in much wider relations. At other times the feeling has arisen from a wish to protect certain cherished convictions from inroads—like those of a barbarous horde—coming from remote and unfamiliar quarters. The defenders of a given form of faith have hoped to build a wall about it not to be scaled by any enemy.

The error is the same, whether we shut in a region of inquiry as sufficient unto itself, or shut one out as barren and unprofitable. We should rather, in our explorations, having the whole world before us, be most pressed, like the Arctic adventurers, in our thought by the things least known. Religion cannot reject the criticisms of science as not pertinent to its high subject-matter, nor can science confidently pursue its own inquiries with a scorn of all conclusions not reached in a like way. These assertions of exclusion imply, whether made in behalf of science or philosophy or religion, or against science or philosophy or religion, either that our field of knowledge is much more circumscribed than we have supposed it to be, or that it is divided into parts, first alien, then hostile, to each other. To these conceptions we oppose that of the unity of knowledge, its exhaustless nature and perpetual expansion.

The differences in the several departments of inquiry have been so exaggerated that they have ceased to seem amenable to the same principles. The very separation into departments, as in so many other cases of classification, has been given a significance beyond its proper import. The three leading divisions are science, philosophy, and religion. Though philosophy and religion have constantly affiliated, there has yet been no little jealousy current between them. The devotee of a particular faith has disliked to subject his beliefs to the last speculations of the philosopher; and the philosopher has refused to accept, as beyond further question, the conclusions of religion already attained. Science, as more detached in its pursuits and peculiar in its methods, has greatly added, as against the other two, to this sense of division. Of late years we have heard more of the diversity of knowledge than of its unity, more of one method of inquiry as excluding other methods than of their reconciliation in a common and complex service.

Laying emphasis on prominent *differentiæ*, we may define descriptively the department of knowledge which we call science as that of physical phenomena collated by causes. We may define philosophy as the phenomena of consciousness collated by reasons, justified comprehensively to themselves; and religion, as the facts of a spiritual world accepted in continuation and explanation of the facts, sensuous and supersensuous, of our present form of existence. Under these definitions of broad contrast, science prepares the way for philosophy, and both make way for religion. The facts of the world, sensuously apprehended, appeal to the reason of man for their widest interpretation; and this interpretation ripens into a belief in a spiritual life which encloses our present life. The mind awakens to its own comprehension, and to the comprehension of the world, as one indivisible process; and in this comprehension it soon finds itself surrounded by a penumbra of spiritual conceptions. Without the three, no one of the three would be vigorously prosecuted for any considerable period. The impulses generated in any one of them carry the mind over, in their fulfilment, into the adjoining fields. We cannot constantly reflect back any movement on itself without slowly destroying it. Any sudden elasticity of inquiry is usually due to its escape into a new field.

In a very general way this is the dependence of the three departments. They are all departments of knowledge; and the knowledge of one flows into, sustains, and corrects that of the other two. This is the unity of the field of thought. These departments have been cultivated in undue independence of one another, and aside from their natural order; and there have been, therefore, corresponding confusion and conflict in the results. But this is a transient fact, due to awkward and inadequate methods. The true method, like knowledge itself, is an object of discovery.

The facts of the external world cannot be broadly considered without giving rise to many suggestions which they themselves do not answer. The mind can no more forego these suggestions than it could its first inquiry. They are all fibres of one root. The solution of them is later, more uncertain, more variable, but lies as truly in the world as the very first investigation. These successive steps of resolution must lead, have always led, enterprising minds to spiritual beliefs, later links in the chain of thought. The whole chain holds together or grows weak together. Taken collectively, it gives a firm and comprehensive attachment of our complex lives to the universe in which we are. We are entitled to the whole of it for the same reason that we are entitled to any part of it. Nothing less than the whole of it can subserve, or ever has subserved, the purposes of our physical, intellectual, and spiritual being.

The extreme difference in these three departments lies between science and religion, while philosophy is the pivotal point on which they are balanced. Let us look a little more exactly at this relation. A system of philosophy underlies, in a latent way, all science, precisely as it underlies all experience. Our philosophy, good or bad, aims simply to render our experience in terms of reason. Our daily experience, and our science as well, come to us in terms of matter and of mind, as causes and reasons; and we fall into no pit simply because we raise no questions as to the nature and validity of these distinctions. If we should undertake to lay aside in use the distinctions themselves, our knowledge would collapse as suddenly as a tent whose cords we had cut. As long as sensuous facts are distinguished from supersensuous ones,—the phenomena of matter from the phenomena of mind—we shall have laid upon us the relation of these two to each other, and the rational renderings of them which keep them apart.

As a fact, therefore, very many distinguished scientists, whose faculties have been thoroughly awakened, are constantly raising philosophical and religious questions. They differ only from those who primarily devote themselves to these inquiries in the form of the answer they give them. They become philosophers, and are to be judged as philosophers. The simple scientist is one who accepts bodily the popular philosophy, and raises no questions against it.

The scientist carries forward his investigations under resources of knowledge, and a discipline of mind, much of which has been secured in connection with philosophy. Philosophy, barren as many of its speculations may seem to have been, has been the intellectual gymnasium of the world. No wise man will think that without its awakenings, its tentative efforts, men would have found their way successfully into empirical inquiry. The notions of causation and of law, while they have been made far more explicit by science, have gone before science, and been its first terms. The inductive logic has not itself been a product of induction, but of reflective thought. Men like John Stuart Mill, of a philosophical habit of mind, have furnished it as a formal system, while as a practical power it has arisen in the rational depths of every sound experience. A mind not full of philosophy can no more give clear reflection to scientific conceptions than roiled waters can yield a well-defined image.

Evolution Unifies Knowledge. 33

The light which has searched out the world has come aslant from the spaces above the world.

We ought not to expect that science should be as directly associated with religion as is religion with science. Science, as a primary kind of knowledge, gives form to later convictions rather than receives form from them; yet in two respects science plainly suffers from the absence of a wise spiritual temper. The physical world has its spiritual suggestions. The mind must be open to them, or it puts upon itself a good deal of barren work. Take, as an example, the presence of final causes. It is not the office of science, in any high degree, to trace these causes; it is rather its habit of mind, in the assiduous pursuit of efficient causes, to neglect them. If, however, it accepts a presumption against them, and studiously rules them out, it as certainly drops into a narrow, predisposed method as if it had undertaken to establish them in any given form. A light which comes only from the rear casts deep, unsoftened shadows, and prevents the world from appearing exactly what it is—luminous on many sides.

If, moreover, science sets itself the task of shutting out the spiritual side of our lives, its results, however accurate they may be in themselves, will meet with less fortunate social uses. The evils and darkness of the social world, like mists and clouds in the sky, will slowly settle down upon inquiry, and shut it out from its own proper work. Science, as a movement of mind, must have its own adequate impulses, its proper inspirations. That inspiration is not simply truth, but truth as the food of the spirit. Here, with the spirit of man, is the ultimate consumption of all intellectual good; and this appetite must in all ways be nourished as the only adequate and permanent incentive to action. A wholesome, invigorating atmosphere can come to the student of nature—and without it he is sooner or later asphyxiated—only from the entire field of knowledge, the field in which truth is put to its highest and most rewardful uses.

If we turn to the other extreme, religion, this dependence of the departments of knowledge on each other is still more obvious. We have in religion no phase of thought that can with any show of reason declare itself independent. The fundamental conceptions in faith are those of the being, nature, and character of God. The data from which we form and establish these conceptions are given us in science and in philosophy, in the facts of the physical and moral world. Whether we regard these proofs as satisfactory or unsatisfactory, there are none other; and so the very foundations of belief repose on the soil of the world, and its entire superstructure is enveloped in its atmosphere. No positive personal revelation can successfully contradict this testimony of the facts of our lives to the attributes of God. The world, as the antecedent, comprehensive fact of divine creation, must easily carry with it in interpretation all its subsequent parts. We can get no standpoint for religion, either physical or spiritual, outside of these phenomena, which completely envelop us. Any one who should declare to us other things than those which are to be found in the record of events, would speak in an unknown tongue. A most striking feature in the teaching of Christ was a ready and constant reflection of spiritual lessons in physical events. His ever-returning parables made the two worlds flow together as text and illustration in one movement of thought. Physical things seemed only the predetermined reflection of spiritual things.

Neither can any dogma or rite or discipline of religion establish successfully any intellectual training or ethical schooling that is not in harmony with the nature of man as played upon by its physical and social circumstances. This has been tried again and again, as in asceticism, and has come to nought. As long as we conceive the world, the flesh, and the devil as alien to men, we fight a losing battle in reference to the Kingdom of Heaven. Our victories must be achieved with and through the forces which enclose us. The whole creation travails together, and together waits on redemption. It is true that the individual may find a spiritual discipline under narrow and faulty conditions, but that discipline largely lies in slowly casting them off. No matter how many convulsive changes and millenniums religion may promise itself, we see that they do not come. Our Christian faith, amid all its prophetic gleams, has travelled a weary road of discipline, in which nothing has been gained save in the slowest, most empirical method. It is utterly in vain that our religious beliefs contradict nature: nature still has her own way. Man can no more rise above the spiritual world to which he belongs, or declare himself independent of it, than the fish can swim without water or the bird fly without air.

We can, then, in no way establish three departments of knowledge whose conclusions are even proximately indifferent to one another. The religionist cannot say, "I accept science in its own field, but I warn it off from the field of faith." No more can the scientist say, "I busy myself with the verifiable facts of the world, all beyond these is changeable and illusory, a province I have no occasion to enter." The body is no more dependent on the mind, and the mind no more dependent on the body, and both no more dependent on the service of the world to them, than are our forms of thought on one another.

A second attempted separation of these departments is made to rest on the facts which they concern. Science pertains to present, physical, and natural events. Religion pertains to future, spiritual, and supernatural events. Religion is a revelation, and must be discussed in its own light. Science is a disclosure of a certain narrow class of things as they lie about us, and aims at no transformation of them.

There are two sufficient answers to this

method of regarding the subject. The dogmas of faith—confining our attention to Christianity, and the case is still stronger if we go beyond it—are very diverse between themselves, are the remote and inferential product of the Scriptures, and have suffered the repeated and painful elaboration of the human mind. If we were to admit all that is claimed in behalf of the Oracles as divine, still these conflicting beliefs remain to be substantiated with no little interpretation, no light criticism, no obscure philosophy. As offered to us, they are shaped by theological thought in every, part of them; in every part of them have met with acceptance or rejection, according to a bias of mind. The facts before us are not a plain, perspicuous revelation on the one side, and doubtful speculation on the other, but universal speculation everywhere. The assumption of a distinct and final revelation is a pure assumption, which each phase of faith makes in its own behalf and against every other phase.

The moment we enter on the common work of criticism, and a doctrinal construction subject to criticism, we can by no possibility keep science and philosophy and religion apart. We oftentimes content ourselves with a very general definition of doctrine—as, for example, the doctrine of inspiration—simply because we cannot construct a more full and explicit one which will bear successfully the criticism of science and philosophy. We have made our words thin and shadowy, that we may thereby become invulnerable.

Shall we call historical criticism a science, or a philosophy? It pertains to sensuous facts, but it does not treat them on their sensuous side. It has as much to do with reasons as with causes, and often proceeds on those subtle estimates of human nature, of spiritual phenomena and ethical method, which pertain to religion. The irreligious nature can hardly yield a sound criticism of Biblical history, any more than an inartistic mind can give us an instructive rendering of a work of art. No more can the intensely religious nature do this work well. Yet historical criticism we must have. Take the Scriptures in their supernatural and natural material, with all the concessions and all the claims of faith upon them, and we have still to frame out of them, with only the ordinary resources of thought, a coherent and intelligible belief. We know full well how East and West, in scores of distinct symbols, this work has been done and undone according to the prevalent philosophy, and how it remains to be redone as we acquire a more direct and empirical outlook on the events with which these spiritual beliefs are interlaced. We have, then, no rendering of religious belief which has, as contrasted with other beliefs, any certain claim to authority.

Not only is criticism very much divided in its results: the religious facts of the world to which it pertains do not lie apart and distinguishable. They are not given by themselves as of their own order: they are united to other facts of every variety of mundane character. We may span a river without a pier; but if we drop midway a support, we must be prepared to encounter the undermining current. The claim of complete inspiration, taking under its protection the physical facts associated with revelation, has given way; and its failure should admonish us that religious truth is nowhere offered to us disassociated with other truth, and safely poised within itself. It is always fully involved in the complex flow of events.

The attack on miracles, regarded as pivotal

points in faith, arose no more from science than from philosophy. It was the very uses of the miracle in the mind itself that gave way. The evidence of science is simply negative. It does not find in nature an *analogon* of the facts associated with revelation. If there was nothing in the supernatural facts themselves to embarrass the mind, this testimony of science would be comparatively weak. Philosophy enters in to make the solution of the supernatural most difficult. Philosophy grounds itself on the coherence of reason with itself, its wise uniformity of method. It is in attempting to learn the lesson involved in the miracles that we meet our chief embarrassment—an embarrassment we cannot shake off, as it arises within the religious life itself. We are admonished of the credulity and folly associated in human history with miracles; the impossibility of accepting this tendency, in the minds of men, to ill-grounded belief, with no purifying process of thought; the extended mischief within the Christian system which has attended on this facility of faith. Religion cannot handle its own statements without raising, concerning them, all the questions of science and philosophy.

We are not attempting to resolve this great problem: we are only drawing attention to the fact that this particular pier, the miracle, which was built up in mid-stream to support the lofty highway of religious belief, chanced to rest where the current has proved strongest and most treacherous. We did not get above the danger by means of it, but into the midst of it. We cannot always remain in the air; and the moment we touch water or land, we must be ready to encounter the urgent conditions of the case before us. Because religion offers us such a variety of facts essential to its later conclusions, science and philosophy, and religion itself, lay hold of these facts, and test them in every way as to the uses to which they are to be put. So it ought to be, so it must be. Nothing can by any possibility touch the world of matter, touch the world of mind, without encountering their laws. Each thing is there for that very purpose. These lines of contact may have for us a very discouraging vagueness, but they are not for that reason less truly interesting. They are like the magnetic poles of the earth—centres of very fugitive but very potent forces.

A separation is sometimes attempted between religious truth and other forms of truth by the assertion that man is possessed of certain powers of apprehension which find exclusive play in the religious world. If this assertion were true, we might see in it a ground for a fundamental division. Spiritual convictions would fall off from secular knowledge as colors separate themselves from sounds. Faith is frequently made this supersensuous power. Consciousness is sometimes given such an extension as to render it an organ of direct approach to God. Occasionally an intuitive faculty is asserted, having the range of the spiritual world. These assertions lack probability, and lack proof. They lack probability, because a religious life which rests on exceptional powers, or powers in an exceptional stage of development, would be so divorced from the life we are now leading as to become quite estranged from it. Indeed, this result has been frequently accepted, and, when not declared, has been involved in the doctrines of election, regeneration, reprobation. All minds do not feel the infinite improbability of this casting-off of the mass of men by the world and by God,—this cutting into distinct and unlike parts the seamless web of life,—but the philosophical instinct of the human mind does feel it, and rises up in rejection of it. Continuity is the very substance of thought and of life ; and continuity in the highest things is affirmed with the accumulated force of reason gathered in the entire field of knowledge.

This distinction of powers utterly lacks proof. Faith—trust in persons, trust in the processes of thought—is a tendency which every man has occasion to watch over. Those who claim an intuition of God have no other revelation to make of him than that with which we are all familiar. Guided by experience, we deny, in the self-elected to light, any new phenomena—any superiority of power, any transcendency in virtue—which need in explanation the alleged additional resources. If we cannot ourselves fly, we should at least be glad to see those who do fly ; and as yet, to the candid and thoughtful mind, they remain invisible. We assert this identity of endowment not in derogation, but in exaltation, of human worth. We know of no psychology of saint or sinner which indicates anything more than the use or the neglect of powers the same for all. All ways are open to us, and all ways are closed to us, according as we are disposed to pursue them.

Another line of demarcation between departments of inquiry has been found in the methods of reasoning employed in them. Inductive methods predominate in science; deductive ones, in philosophy and religion. This difference is often exaggerated, and then regarded as fundamental. The real advantage of physical facts over intellectual ones as subjects of inquiry is found in their greater simplicity and permanency of form. Our senses return to us phenomena whose variations are much less rapid and obscure than are the changes in the shifting experiences of consciousness. There is, therefore, a sense of stability which accompanies the one series of impressions, and is unattainable by the other. This stability gives ease in the use of induction in physical inquiries, and the want of it embarrasses the mind in the pursuit of intellectual law.

There is, however, no distinction in these departments of thought which makes induction peculiar to one, or deduction to another. The two forms of logic are freely commingled in every investigation. There is scarcely more than one kind of knowledge that is exclusively dependent on one kind of reasoning; and that knowledge is pure mathematics, built up by deduction. In this instance, at least, deduction shows no inferiority in the certainty of its results to the highest attainments of induction. Any reasoning which pertains to facts, and not to the pure forms of thought, must contain both inductive and deductive elements—induction as putting us in possession of the facts, and deduction as making that possession fruitful. The breadth and stability of our knowledge turn not on the one or the other form of thought, but on the skill with which both are employed. It is impossible to escape this admission, unless we assert, with Mill, that all deduction is disguised induction. In that case, we are far out in the swim of metaphysics, and it is a question which concerns ourselves chiefly, what shore we shall reach, or whether we shall reach any shore.

If we use words as men use them, we shall see that science does not rest exclusively on induction, nor religion on deduction. Knowledge is not a matter of the senses simply, no more is it of the forms of thought taken by themselves. The senses give us the material of knowledge, which the mind unfolds. The relations, and the things between which the relations hold, constitute inseparable parts of our convictions. Not till we have gathered the facts together in a wise induction do we get the safe footing of thought; not till we pass beyond this footing, carrying our conclusions with us, do we experience the expansive, guiding power of truth. Induction is for deduction, deduction is the fruition of induction.

A deduction closely associated with induction, and which everywhere goes with it, is the conviction of the uniformity of nature—that a conclusion good for one set of facts is good for all similar facts; that the truths of to-day are also those of to-morrow. This ever-present postulate of inquiry is the deductive fruit of that primitive conviction that like causes are followed by like effects. The intimate way in which induction and deduction thus touch each other and confirm each other, serves only to show what essential parts they are of one vital movement of mind. No induction can cover any considerable part of the facts to which it pertains. It is impossible to push any induction to a finish; and we make no effort to do so, because we are aware that shortly it entitles us to a rapid and safe deduction. We carry the inquiry further, or stop sooner, according to the complexity of the causes with which we are dealing, and our certainty that we have grasped them in their own nature. The moment we are sure that we have in hand the forces involved in the inquiry, we desist from further examination as superfluous. We have then fallen on the paths of reason. The simplicity and stability of physical facts make this limit more quickly attainable in science, and leave us sooner free for a new inquiry.

Nor is this constant expansion of our premises the only deductive force of mind present in induction. Empirical inquiries always imply a separation of phenomena—a reference of them by parts to different causes; a tracing, amid complex sensuous appearances, of certain results that are thought to be dependent on each other. Now, this anticipatory, elective movement, on which the fruitfulness of observation and experiment is dependent, is of a deductive order. It is seeing where probable dependencies are to be found, what things involve each other. The skilful inquirer is never in a simply sensuous state of mind, but in an exceedingly active, penetrating one, directing his attenton to the pregnant facts. The movement of mind is from within outwards rather than from with-

Evolution Unifies Knowledge. 49

out inwards. The informing force, therefore, of induction is always deduction—a following of the clews of thought. The corrective tendency in deduction is induction; and this fact leads us, not to a distinction in subject-matter between physical and spiritual inquiries, but to a difference in the ease with which the two elements of knowledge, the outer fact and its intellectual law, are combined. In religious thought we are often as one who entertains a beautiful vision and refuses to open his eyes lest it should be dissipated.

In matters of faith, deductive guidance is more extended; inductive correction, more remote and obscure: hence we have often allowed the one to proceed quite too independently of the other, and have lost our way among empty and detached speculations. Spiritual beliefs are as certainly subject to inductive confirmation as are the conclusions of science. If we are dealing in thought with the government of God, the nature of man, the regenerative processes in the human spirit, the corrective powers in the spiritual world, phenomena appropriate to the inquiry are everywhere about us. If we construct our dogmatic theories in oversight of the facts, we do it with a certain inexcusable wilfulness. If we affirm that the heart of man is perfectly perverse, and his mind wholly blind to spiritual truth, we are in neglect of things very near to us in our daily life. We override our experience by a theory concerning it, instead of framing our theory in immediate reference to it. If we declare that God cannot freely forgive sin, it is because we have not recognized that inductive law which is established by observing the results of forgiveness among men. The many mistakes of religion prove the likeness of the two fields, that induction must accompany and correct deduction as certainly in spiritual as in physical things. The difference between them is not one of kind, but of degree; is found in the more fugitive and perplexed form of intellectual phenomena. An inductive epoch is being entered on in religious inquiry, and is becoming fruitful in many directions. Look on science, philosophy, and religion as we will, we shall find diversity, not division, between them. They are parts of one kingdom of truth, not distinct kingdoms subject to wholly different laws. The affirmation of the unity of all knowledge is nothing more than an assertion of the omnipresence of causes and reasons. The impulse which leads us to concede a cause at all must lead us to concede it universally: if we once ask for a reason, we must ask for it again and again. There are no planes of cleavage which these movements of mind may not traverse.

This union between all forms of knowledge in subject-matter, in method of inquiry, in the aid and correction they bring each other, is established beyond denial by the doctrine of evolution. Evolution is a movement which extends through all fields, is continuous in all, and completed by all. It is a living current which threads its way across every shallow and by every lagoon, drawing their waters with greater or less rapidity into the one river.

Physical evolution, long and bright as are the stretches by which it has come down to us, has measurably reached its destination. Looking at the very superior and complex structure of man, we are not prepared to see it displaced in the lead of life by any new physical organization. There is no indication of such a result in the facts before us. The body of man may be greatly improved in power, but it suggests a limit to physical refinements rather than a promise to take them up at some new point.

Trees that are rooted in a soil much the same forever, and that are to encounter ever-returning storms, find therein a boundary of development. Nervous tissue, subject to the gross stimuli of the physical world, cannot take on all phases of sensibility. There is an ultimate fitness of relation which defines itself and arrests movement as we approach it. We do not see, therefore, how this stream, beginning to be shut in and to head back on itself, can renew its flow in the physical world simply. When, however, we put in place of physical life, social and spiritual life, the current at once shows new force. It pours over the present barriers, seeks remote places, and takes possession of distant periods. We are just at the beginning of intellectual life ; and we must give it in evolution, as its latest and highest product, all the significance which belongs to it. Where evolution has placed it, the fruit of one stage and the germinant force of another, we must place it. What evolution puts highest is highest by an ordination which runs back to the very beginning.

Evolution is not simply continuity, it is development. As man's physical structure, in reference to animal life, is a goal, so also is the perfecting of human society a goal in reference to human history and all the races of men. It is at once continuation and diversity, movement and consummation. Evolution involves equally both notions. The movement is not aimless, the aim is not foreign to the movement. We should feel the full implication of evolution. It does not overwhelm us with physical forces, it marshals them all for our largest service.

The transition we are making from the physical to the spiritual world as the chief seat of incentives, while it is a bold one, is also one of the closest genetic dependence and of the most comprehensive and inclusive sweep. Nothing is neglected, nothing left behind. The physical and the spiritual are built together as one kingdom,—a kingdom that we can declare to be neither physical nor spiritual, but both ; each in the other in an indivisible fashion, as inspiration and elevation in a cathedral. The science of the world and the art of the world cohabit in one home,—a home whose resources are just beginning to be developed. The fine art of the world and the spiritual life of the world are born into this household as at once of it and beyond it, the fruit of one living movement.

Though the simple fact that the social powers of men rest wholly back on the physical forces of the world, that these forces thus mount up into a spiritual realm quite beyond them,—as a plant of rugged stem and prickly leaf suddenly breaks out in a flower of transcendent form and color—is so evident and so wonderful as to make evolution the crowning law of the universe, it does not express all that is contained in that idea as bringing into harmony the several departments of our lives and making our knowlege identical and forceful in every part of it. It was this unity we started to enforce.

The two elements in the world which we find equally indispensable in our apprehension of it, but in reconciling which we also meet with much difficulty, are matter and mind. Though the world itself shows no plane of cleavage between them, men are constantly splitting it into parts along this line of analysis. The vision of men, like Iceland spar, polarizes the light, and gathers its sundered rays at distinct centres. A philosophy of heroic methods strives to subject mental processes to the laws of physical processes, or it labors hard to gather up all physical connections into mental ones. Only at rare and sane intervals is it content to accept the world as it finds it—an equilibrium of the two in one indivisible product. Evolution as a law helps us at this point. While it makes neither the materialistic nor the idealistic tendency impossible, it discloses, through long periods, their reciprocal correction of each other, and the growing interlock of physical and intellectual forces in knowledge. It declares for neither. They have, in development, sustained from time to time a different balance in reference to each other; but they have both been uniformly present. The increasing refinements of the material world have served to make it an ever more perfect medium of mind. The physical terms have preceded the intellectual ones, and prepared the way for them. The mental element does not offer itself as a simple, uniform ingredient of matter, but as one steadily superinduced upon it, united with it under the processes of evolution. Evolution distinguishes the two terms of experience, emphasizes their constructive relation to each other, and pushes the mind forward in anticipation to a still more perfect interplay. It shows no tendency to merge the one in the other, or make less bold their contrast. The world never ceases to be physical, or ceases to be intellectual, but embraces, in its progressive unfolding, more completely both elements.

In our analysis of the powers of mind, there has been a disposition to attach a validity to sensuous perception, which has not been conceded to the rational ideas which accompany it. Some who accept color and form are stumbled by forces and causes. In evolution, however, the sensuous and the rational renderings are offered as one indivisible product of growth. Evolution gives no confirmation to the distinction we may make in favor of sense-perception. Its movement towards knowledge includes, and by including establishes, both ingredients. We might as well disparage instincts in animals, as compared with appetites, because the instinct has a less definite physical basis, as to think slightingly of the forms of reason in contrast with their sensuous content. Evolution, as one whole, discloses this very tendency of reaching terms ever more supersensuous, and of carrying its movement forward by means of them. This progressiveness is of the very substance of evolution. It brings the higher to the lower as certainly as it proffers the lower to the higher. Knowledge is the product of an indivisible fascicle of powers that have grown up on one disc. Better, these powers are the organs of one flower, productive by means of them all.

Allied to this contention between physical and rational terms is that between the natural and the supernatural, of whose strife, whose inclusions and exclusions, human thought is now full. Evolution, advancing along a line of exposition, has drawn freely from the right and the left, from sensuous and supersensuous sources, for its explanatory material. The expository movement is taking on a marked change in this respect. The supernatural is coming to stand in a different relation to the natural from that which it has hitherto held. Evolution serves to unite and to explain these successive, yet contrasted, positions. There is a unity between them in spite of their diversity. There are a dependence between them, and a needfulness of both, which make of them a necessary sequence in the growth of knowledge—parts of one evolutionary process. What we are really occupied with is, not the exclusion of the supernatural, but its more perfect inclusion, its better definition and its harmony with the natural. Under the earlier exposition, they displaced each other with much conflict and jar; under the later exposition, they are coming to glide into each other along the lines which unite physical and spiritual phenomena. What the supernaturalist has been contending for from the very beginning has been spiritual forces, though he saw not how wisely to unite them to physical ones. What the naturalist contends against is that method of use, on the part of his opponent, which makes the supernatural an alien element, displacing and disturbing natural law.

This has been the pivot on which the ever-returning discussion of miracles has hinged. If every miracle as a simple event were yielded as lacking adequate proof, the fundamental principles of the spiritual world would remain what they are. Nor can our grasp of these principles be truly satisfactory and vital till we find them for ourselves in the very familiar phenomena to which they pertain. When we have so secured them, we have no longer any need that any one should tell us of them, or establish them in any wonderful way, for we ourselves have discovered them in their true form.

Miracles, as mere facts, are not worth the contention they have occasioned, can in no way make good the position which has been assigned them. Nay, more, we may well affirm that the denial of them has been none too earnest and decided, looked on as a means of correcting this wrong relation to revelation which has been assigned them. Men have sought for a sign, and, having found what they have deemed a sign, they have diverted their attention from the truth to a relatively sensuous pursuit of its symbols. They have followed the star, but it has not come to rest over the babe in Bethlehem. What we profoundly and constantly need is a knowledge of the laws of the spiritual world, and not some meteoric flash that may seem for a moment to dispel the darkness, but leaves us, in the end, more confused than ever.

Are we, then, to set down this universal and protracted movement in the thoughts of men as fruitless wandering? Have men merely lost the path, and are they now being restored to it? We cannot answer these questions with a simple affirmative in consistency with the laws of evolution. Men as one whole do not lose their way, any more than a river misses its channel. The path pursued may be a tedious and circuitous one; but it is a certain one, and there is none other. The thing contended for in the miracle, and for the time being won for the masses of men, was a spiritual presence in the world. If, in yielding the miracle, we should yield this presence, we should suffer irretrievable loss. The constructive law of the world is found in that equilibrium which men had in view in affirming the supernatural as well as the natural. The spirit cannot save itself for its own uses without saving that which it has held fast by means of the miracle. The spirit of man cannot win the world as a suitable medium of its own powers, without implications allied to those of the miracle. If we accept the miracle at once, we are involved in a hopeless accumulation of superstitions. If we deny it at once, on scientific grounds simply, we cut ourselves off from the inner spiritual power of the world. We need as spiritual beings both the causes and reasons which penetrate our lives—both the settled order and the upward tendency through that order. Thus only does the world reflect back upon us our own lives, and nourish, as one vital plexus, our thoughts, our actions, and our affections. We must hold fast to the world as a medium of divine life. This is its profoundest rendering.

What has been accomplished by this discussion is a shifting of ground, not toward naturalism as a finality, but toward a more complete recognition of both elements, and a more adequate adjustment of them to each other. If God is immanent in the world, he need in no way transcend the world, working it forward according to his will. The spirit of man —so we believe—rules in the body of man, but it does it under the general form of physical law. If the attack on miracles is made to mean that the world is a mechanical world, one of quantities and qualities adequate to a certain work and wholly unable to go beyond it, then the spirit must confront it in a struggle for its own existence. There is no obscurity of thought admissible here. We must have a vital world, a world with a spiritual atmosphere, or we must be left to perish—vermin under an exhausted receiver—in a dead world. We can no more survive in a mechanical world than we can live in a tomb. All we think, all we do, all we hope, all we fear, presuppose a pliant, spiritual protoplasm in which processes of life and death are potentially present.

We must save the whole or we cannot save the parts. If God is powerless, locked up in the ruts of law, much more are we powerless. If we have power, infinitely more has God power. There is no such lamination between the physical and the spiritual, that, dividing them, we can yield the one to causes, and retain the other for reasons. Causes, passing an invisible line, become reasons; and reasons, returning by the same path, reveal themselves as causes. It has well been said that if God cannot intervene in the physical world, no more can he in the spiritual world. He cannot answer prayer, though it be directed to a spiritual state. The spiritual and the physical are too closely interlaced to allow us to handle either in disconnection from the other. We approach the physical through the spiritual, and the spiritual through the physical. We persuade and dissuade, we sway each other in many ways, but we do it by the intervention of physical media. To suppose that God influences our minds aside from their surrounding is a harsh supposition, of the same nature as that which condemns the miracle. Like it, it will certainly disappear.

Freedom is involved in the very fact of

thought. It is the truth that makes us free. The mind and the truth are in reciprocal interaction. The mind pursues the truth, the truth renews for the mind changeable conditions of activity. The relation is a free one. No man can enforce his opinion on any other supposition than that of a real, yet variable, affinity between thought and truth. But if we admit liberty, we admit it as a constructive term in the universe, physical and spiritual. With it comes not simply the freedom of man with the world, but the freedom of man with God and of God with man. This, the higher half of liberty, throbs with constructive power. Our Lord's Prayer is wonderful in its recognition alike of the steadfast movement and the incessant modification. The Kingdom is to come in its own grand way, we are to have nourishment, forgiveness, protection; but it is to be done part by part, day by day, the presence of God the supreme fact in it all.

What evolution has done and is doing is to secure a re-adjustment of the natural and the supernatural to each other, a better conception of both, and a more perfect interplay between them. This perpetual re-adjustment makes evolution true to itself. The turnings to the right and the turnings to the left are the bendings of the river, subject, from fountain to mouth, to the same cosmic impulse. We come to see that we ourselves—as we well may be under evolution—are *analogons* of the universe; that both elements, the natural and the supernatural, the causal and the free, are in us; that they are in systematic, growing interaction, and that no miracle is involved simply because a constructive method gives no occasion for it. This discussion of miracles is only one phase of the equally persistent and illusive discussion of human freedom.

It follows from the doctrine of development, as applied to man's religious nature, that no phase of belief is in any sense absolute. No generation submits itself, in matters of faith, to any previous generation, nor is itself a law to any subsequent one. The spiritual conceptions at any moment current are in harmony with the renderings of the facts of the world with which they are associated. As these change, those must change with them. The two together make a coherent, intellectual whole. The external facts and the internal interpretations of our lives are reciprocally

Evolution Unifies Knowledge.

causes and effects, as much so as are physical surroundings and vital powers. We are no more wise in putting on earlier forms of faith our more subtile spiritual impressions than we are in submitting these, our more expansive thoughts, to their rendering of the facts. The question thus becomes, in reference to the earlier church and miracles, not what part do miracles now play in our belief, but what part did they then play in the powerful spiritual life then present? The followers of Christ interpreted current events under the formulæ familiar to them; and what we are perfectly sure of is, that this rendering was a highly vital process with them. The old, in its time and way, was as instructive and progressive as the new, in its time and way.

If we take such an event as the resurrection of Christ, it is impossible to believe that the disciples, confounded and spiritually overthrown as they were by the crucifixion, rallied on a purely spiritual basis, saw that Christ remained in the highest possible sense the way, the truth, and the life, and yet were led to sustain their position so achieved, with what would then have been the legendary trumpery of the resurrection. Our theological growth carries with it our theological sentiments. We are repugnant to miracles because miracles are repugnant to our conceptions. With the earlier Christians, spiritual insight and a marvellous rendering of events were one and the same thing. They construed the world, and the world instructed them, as indicated in the Gospels. That experience of miracles which we so sharply criticise has undeniably been a most salutary and wholesome training to many persons in spiritual life, an inseparable constituent in a truly vital movement.

The question then assumes this form, Is it probable that a perfectly practical, searching, and sober faith—such as was that of the earlier Christians—was interwoven with a conception of facts which was fanciful and fictitious throughout? Are the actual and the spiritual in this way divorced from each other? If so, what becomes of our notion of evolution? In place of it, we are, under our own standards, affirming an absolute character in things and thoughts. A Gospel so elastic as to be just entering, in our time, on its true government is deeply involved in an entire misconstruction of the world. It is not, on this supposition, with a partial rendering, but with a misrendering, that we have to do. Does the physical world lie, in reference to the spiritual world that is growing upon it and expanding over it, in this eternally dead and irresponsive attitude?

Our theism—for this discussion presupposes theism—must lead us more and more into a Divine Personal Presence; must make worship, prayer, trust, rest, the inevitable outcome of our lives. If the world is for us increasingly vitalized by the omnipresence of God, can we reject, in a dogmatic, final way, those very conceptions by which the race has climbed into this belief? A belief in miracles, as an expression of a Divine Presence, came nearer to our present faith than would have been a rejection of miracles in behalf of a framework of things impenetrable to the Divine Mind. We must explain each successive phase of life by its own inner forces, and by the lines of succession in which it lies. It is not by any perfection of parts at any one time that we interpret the world under the notion of evolution, but by its coherence in a changeable, forward movement. If we admit the world to be both physical and spiritual in a thoroughly interpenetrative way, then the interplay of the two on each other and under each other will alter with successive stages of development. Neither is complete in reference to the other. The two are passing into a harmony ever deeper, more restful, more masterful. The first condition of spirituality is that we do not suffer the physical to overpower the intellectual, that we allow the intellectual to find its way ever more completely into the physical. We cannot start this movement by a flat denial of its first steps.

We have referred to the constant separation in thought of physical and intellectual elements, and the passionate pursuit of one or another type of monism, in a vain hope of identifying the two. This tendency repeats itself in a great variety of ways, calling out some new phase of strife between the form and the inner force of things. Pleasing manners are separated from good-will with more or less friction between them. Style in composition is cultivated somewhat aside from the idea to be conveyed. Realism in the novel is made to take the place of a disclosure of the spiritually constructive forces in life. Rhythm in the poem is sought with no close affiliation of sentiment. August religious ceremonial is made a primary expression of the religious life. The deepest form of this division is present in putting sequence in place of causation; the phenomena of life for life itself; an associative order in men's thoughts for the power of thought; and the exterior inductions of experience, in themselves half instinctive, for the inner revelation of reason.

So universal and persistent a disposition on the part of the two constituents of truth to break the bonds of affinity, and let the mind fall back on a more elementary experience, is very significant, both as a fact and in the inevitable correction which comes to it. Evolution brings light at this point. This separation takes place between sensuous and spiritual impressions, the familiar external form and the less familiar internal force, because this is the transition we are now making in growth. The sensuous life, with difficult gestation, is passing into the spiritual life. The two elements are achieving a permanent organic fellowship under the ever-growing power of the superior tendency. One might liken the transition to the chemical unions constantly formed, and as constantly lost again, under the fierce heat which attended on the earlier construction of the globe. We see also why the thoughts are quickly brought back to the inner element, as an essential term of comprehension, no matter in how many ways they wander from it. This is the barrier to be cleared; and the mind, like a restive steed, is restored to it with a short turn.

Evolution not only discloses a reason for this persistent conflict in knowledge, it corrects it. Our conclusions are found to be superficial and unsatisfactory unless they are made to recognize this growing spiritual force. The soil of physical facts must show its fertility by becoming the seed-bed of rare intellectual life or we soon lose even its lower uses. Knowledge, and the higher service of knowledge cannot, for any considerable period, be separated from each other. This fact arises from the truly organic character of the mind. Its affections must have concurrent expression in action with its thoughts, or both lose impulse. A few may push inquiry or speculation very far, and find a sufficient motive in the pleasure of unexpended powers. But this activity exhausts itself unless the ground in the rear comes to be spread over and occupied by men; unless some strong reaction on the human heart sets in, giving life a permanent footing in the new field. No disproportionate development can sustain itself. Emigration must follow exploration, or the lessons of exploration are soon lost. Knowledge must pass over into the uses of knowledge, and these uses must be adequate, or knowledge itself soon becomes sterile.

This is still move evident when we take into consideration the masses of men. They at no time interest themselves in intellectual activities which return no harvests to the common storehouses. The reason why philosophy became a by-word was chiefly this separation of speculative and practical interests. Bacon brought forward the test of "fruits" as the voice of men at large. Science has had new interests and rewarding inquiries assigned it in exhaustless succession because of the productive powers it has developed. But the most comprehensive uses of knowledge are social, spiritual ones—uses which centre the soul of man within itself and give it restfulness—uses which awaken a genial spirit between men, build them together about a common social purpose, and make of them a kingdom. If knowledge fails us in any one of these uses, as we in due order catch sight of them, we shall turn in all directions till the error is corrected, the way once more found.

Though empirical inquiry has gained astonishing prevalence by falling on a large productive service, it cannot, any more than speculation, sustain itself indefinitely without meeting in due order the demands of the social world. Spiritual life is the final test, simply because it is the completion of the organic circuit. This conception of life, evolution confirms; and this problem of life, evolution comes in to solve. We are building up very slowly, it is true, but with corresponding depth and breadth, a higher social state. In this and by this all our powers will be renewed in direction and widened in purpose. The substance and force of knowledge will become increasingly inseparable. The sensuous will have lost its too tenacious hold on us, and the spiritual will have confirmed itself in an experience as definite and enjoyable as that now associated with physical impulses. The two, by an organic interlock, will reveal their entire unity. The highest uses of knowledge will disclose to us more of the nature of knowledge, and we shall understand that vital force in the divine movement which is bringing together these two terms of a perfected life. What we may call the movement of evolution is also the movement of reason, and the sense of powers increasingly rewardful in their activity.

The world is thus laid open to us as a dynamic, living, spiritual product. The reality, the sensuality, of a physical world, are made to underlie the visions and evanescent aspirations of a spiritual one. The expansive power of a spiritual world enters the inertia and grossness of a physical one. The spirit is clothed, and clothed in a garment suited to its own regal nature. The divisions and the diversities of knowledge disappear under this movement, and its unity is found where alone unity can be found—in a marvellous reconciliation of things far apart and near together. Truth and falsehood, holiness and sin, happiness and suffering, are brought to light and eliminated in one and the same struggle. They are not alien ingredients accidentally commingled, but the reason of each is contained in the other. The universe is an evolution, a travailing in pain, with this burden of life at its heart.

PART III.

EVOLUTION IN ITS PRESENT SPIRITUAL PHASES.

In the stoical period of the Roman Empire, the positive religion had come to be regarded as merely an art for obtaining preternatural assistance in the affairs of life, and the moral amelioration of mankind was deemed altogether external to its sphere.

. . . .

On the one hand, we find a system of Ethics, of which, when we consider the range and beauty of its precepts, the sublimity of the motives to which it appealed, and its perfect freedom from superstitious elements, it is not too much to say, that though it may have been equalled, it has never been surpassed. On the other hand, we find a society almost absolutely destitute of moralizing institutions, occupations, or beliefs, existing under an economical and political system, which inevitably led to general depravity, and passionately addicted to the most brutalizing amusements.—WILLIAM G. H. LECKY, *History of European Morals.*

PART III.

EVOLUTION IN ITS PRESENT SPIRITUAL PHASES.

I.

EVOLUTION implies a movement perfectly coherent in every portion of it. It is one, therefore, which can be traced in all its parts by the mind—one in which we, as intelligent agents, are partakers, first, as diligently inquiring into it; second, as concurrently active under it; and, third, as in no inconsiderable degree modifying its results. This our shaping power is disclosed, as a single example, in the many varieties of plants and animals which are the products of man's intervention. Evolution descends to the minutest particulars, and no sensible gain is out of relation to all that has gone before. Evolution, therefore, is most directly opposed to that form of the creative idea which man derives from his own mechanical work, and then transfers to the divine work. To the possibility of immediate construction, he adds the notion of infinite power, and so is at a loss to understand why the world, on its physical and on its spiritual side, is not made at once to respond to the divine wisdom and the divine grace. This mystery remains insoluble as long as the creative idea expressed in the words, "Let there be light and there was light," is kept in the foreground. Under this conception man's chief spiritual function is that of prayer, his chief grace that of patience, and his chief hope that of divine intervention. The changes of the world are to be great, convulsive; to extend from above downward, and to issue in a new heavens and a new earth.

The mental and spiritual discipline of these two ideas—that of a slow, constant, and perfectly coherent growth; and that of sudden and unforeseen intervention, a thief in the night—is very different. The transition from the one to the other is a difficult and painful one: yet it is plainly a passage from a lower to a higher conception; from waiting on God to working with him; from a relatively blind dependence on inexplicable providences to a perfectly rational co-operation with a wise and comprehensive method; from a confused jumbling of causes and reasons in one tangled skein to a careful extension of them, like a net spread out, till they cover the entire field of thought and action. Like the spider at the centre of its web, the mind moves freely in all directions, and from all receives every intimation of opportunity.

We cannot fail to see how ennobling is this conception of the world which makes it the true habitat of human reason, which opens it out before the mind of man to its utmost circumference, which fills it everywhere with light. Nor can we fail to feel that the world thus becomes the true arena of spiritual life, and must ultimately call out and reward every affection. It commences with the constructive activities of the mind itself. It awakens it thoroughly in its highest rational powers. It puts, and that increasingly, all other powers under its control. It makes a correspondingly luxuriant emotional life come forth from, and rest back upon, this integrity of the spirit. As in the body the most pervasive and permanent pleasures are associated with the most perfect health, so in the mind the most stable and proportionate affections are connected with the largest outlook of reason.

Yet these two conceptions of the world do not grow independently of each other. They each have a false form, and each brings correction to the other. The first idea springs from magnifying personal power, and at the same time robbing it of its own proper law; narrowing it in its resources and cutting it off from any extended action and reaction with the world which expresses its work. The mind first wakes up to itself as a productive agent, carries the notion over to God, and there gives it an expression so positive as to make it in the last degree arbitrary, destructive of all the ways of wisdom which have revealed it, and must still reveal it. The world, on which so much has been expended, is gathered back into the hand of God to be hurled forth in some new direction and in some new way. Thus the child retains by a string the ball it plays with. Nothing is impossible with God. We render these words as equivalent to, " All things are open to him ; nothing has been done once for all ; everything may be done on the instant." We do not see that we thereby annihilate the creative idea, and suffer each successive bubble to collapse on its own centre.

The initiatory idea for man is this feeling of

power and purpose in the world, but it must be immediately followed by a sense of inner law and limitation. This notion of personal, rational power—which is none the less the root idea, the source of all inquiry—first offers itself in an extravagant and contradictory form. Man, from his own power of mechanical construction,—to which he attaches unreasonable importance—arrives at a theory of the world which goes far to overshadow and make void this very notion of personal liberty. God is made to possess the same liberty in so full and unrestrained a form as to leave no room for the liberty of man. The notion of liberty is left so crude that it can co-exist with no other notion, and only in one person at a time. The decrees of God are minute, unyielding, and concede nothing to the devices of men. One of the most painful chapters in human experience has been the struggle of man to reconcile his own liberty with the liberty of God. Liberty, power, going forth from its chief centre, has immediately obliterated all cross-lines, or reduced them to shadowy traces which express no genuine control. This most uncomfortable contradiction between the power of God and the liberty of man, between the strength and scope of the moral government of the world and the impotency of those subject to it, between a theory which left no room for freedom and a stolid assertion of freedom as the initiatory idea of the entire theological system, has been, as in the striking example of Jonathan Edwards, the lurid and dramatic force of a religious life struggling after peace and righteousness, with no peace or righteousness in its own thought of God. The spiritual life has become, under this faith, irreconcilable with itself; not a normal growth to be corrected and enlarged through the conditions which surround it, but a blind struggle of vital impulses with themselves, waiting for some more happy moment—the fever passing by—in which to clear themselves. The total miscarriage of this religious philosophy is seen in the long, dismal, yet most instructive history of asceticism, in which squalor, maceration, and an anarchy of bewildered feeling, took the place of the pleasure and sunlight of God's love.

The problem of growth is always how to achieve a positive advance, and at the same time to make it a true unfolding of present resources. The problem of spiritual growth is how to raise man above the world, and yet to put him in ever more fortunate possession of it. The expansion of the branches of a tree is accompanied by a corresponding extension of its roots downward, and the two movements measure each other. The spiritual life is simply a higher and wider range of motives brought into the entire life. It can no more be perfected without an unfolding of all the forces subject to it than these forces can take on their own true harmony aside from its reconciling guidance.

It is a great thing that men should conceive the possibility of a better life, and should state the problem to themselves, no matter in how inadequate a form and with what misconceptions of method. This vision is the promise of all that follows. The conception of that which is higher, holier, comes to men almost exclusively in the region of religious faith; and that faith, in its manifold failures, has yet ushered into the thoughts of men this aspiration for a fuller possession of themselves. This sense of the need of progress must precede any inquiry into its conditions. The soul thus germinates within itself, and puts forth towards a spiritual world. This is the religious history of man. We have not understood it, because we have not apprehended its essential identity in its several phases; we have accepted only one or another of them as truly significant, and have regarded these favored faiths as possessed of an absolute authority which quite separated them from the general history of the world.

The existing confusion of the religious world is corrected only by the idea of evolution, a slow finding of light by many minds in many directions, a steady development under the light of the common life, making still higher knowledge possible. This conclusion is on the very face of the facts. A hundred forms of faith, each affirming superiority in an absolute way, disprove one another. It is in the highest degree improbable that the authority of any one is what its disciples regard it to be; and improbable, though not in the same degree, that any one of them is wholly without value. The confusion is like that which attends on many conflicting accounts of one transaction. The proof of the correctness of any one of them disappears, and it becomes probable that they have all grown up about some separate features in the event itself. The event is not discredited, the reverse rather, but the specific renderings of it lose authority. In the case of religious beliefs, this absolute assurance arises more frequently from the part assigned revelation; but, as revelation is claimed under so many conflicting forms, the claim itself comes under the general doubt and disturbance.

This estimate of the value of every faith, and of the partial value of any faith, is confirmed when we turn to the possibilities of correct apprehension which belong to the human mind. Anything like absolute and complete truth is impossible to it on any comprehensive subject. Truth means a correspondence of men's thoughts with the real quality of that to which they pertain. There can be no such correspondence in the spiritual world, incident to the very primary and obscure experiences which belong to men in this field. To affirm infallibility in dogma is to affirm infallibility in the mind which entertains it, and that affirmation is in entire oversight of the intellectual and moral conditions of the lives of men.

Truth is a slow development as certainly as is righteousness, and their unfoldings keep step with each other. Virtue is the hold of the feelings on the spiritual world, and truth is the hold of the thoughts on it. Neither hold can be fully attained without the other. Action is the medium of both, is the loom in which the web of experience is woven, its parts slowly bound together. The claim of any adequate and unmistakable truth in the spiritual world is a claim to complete holiness in the same direction. Accept evolution, which lies on the surface of the religious history of the world, and the perplexities of our many and perplexed forms of faith disappear. By error and by truth, by vice and by virtue, men have been corrected, and guided into a higher life. Only as that life becomes their universal experience, and so attains its true dimensions, can it be completely apprehended in thought, feeling, action. The religious life is pre-eminently a social life,—a life of the affections—and for that reason spiritual revelation must gather in and interpret every scrap of human experience.

Under the evolutionary rendering of our religious growth, scepticism and agnosticism play a part by no means unimportant. Scepticism, though it may not well understand its own office, and may often go beyond it, simply compels inquiry to ever renew and enlarge itself. It is the decomposition which accompanies recomposition in growth. It is giving ground by that which is less fit in the presence of that which is more fit. It is the aggressive force of the mind, by which it breaks through error and renews effort.

Agnosticism, though less frequently applicable, serves, in the mining of the veins of knowledge, to close up dangerous shafts, to wall in drifts that have proved unproductive. It is a most important preliminary to well-directed inquiry to understand what we can know, and what we can not know; what, from its very nature, is purely speculative, and what can yield us practical guidance. It is only absolute agnosticism,—a distrust of the knowing process, a putting in its place of sensuous impressions—that is of the nature of paralysis. If we cannot travel beyond our senses above the world, we cannot travel beyond them in the world. The two movements are essentially one. Both proceed by the same clews of thought. When we affirm that the thing which is, has been and shall be,—an assertion at the basis of all induction—we are stepping out firmly on a mental conviction. We are planting ourselves squarely on a first premise of thought, the rational coherence of things. We do nothing more than this when we pass from the physical to the spiritual. The physical contains for us spiritual elements, is full of suggestions and implications. We may well lay hold of them, and give them free expression. If we do this inadequately or inaccurately, we have still obeyed the highest bent of mind, and strengthened it. The mind never can deny itself this outward movement into the unknown. It is of its very substance. Every inference projects the mind beyond its sensuous perceptions. This is that which we know as intellectual power. In induction the examples sensuously present with us are as nothing, as compared with those embraced in the sweep of the law thereby established. Our various forms of reasoning differ from each other in the breadth and security of our premises, but not in the methods by which we transcend them. The mind is one and the same plexus of powers, whether spreading out over sensuous or supersensuous phenomena; whether enclosing, in the sweep of its thought, things, or persons, or divine methods. In these exertions, one and all, it is understanding the world.

The deepest thing involved in this swaying of the mind backward and forward is liberty. The true disclosure is that of a power of its own order, springing up within itself, under its own law. The knowledge of the world and the mastery of the world mean this. Spontaneity in mind is as much the ruling conception in intellectual action as is the plastic power of life in organic products. There is in each living thing a combination of phenomena, which, in their relation to each other, we can interpret in no other way than by this notion of life. The inference is universal and unavoidable. In like manner, the phenomena of knowledge involve reason, guiding itself from within itself to its own conclusions. Without this supposition, these phenomena escape in air like a volatile fluid. To get this conclusion, hold it fast, and learn its limitations, is the work of a long evolutionary process.

If we allow the notion of personal power to pass, on the side of religious belief, into the doctrine of decrees, or, on the side of physical inquiry, into universal causation,—the fatalism of forces hidden in things—the universe becomes unintelligible to us, and unmanageable by us. Our daily experience, and the language in which we are accustomed to render it, are made contradictory to each other. The intellectual heavens we spread over our physical conditions has in it no vitality, sets up with them no actions and reactions, brings to us no incentives, and yields no fresh limitations. It is a painted sky spread over a painted landscape.

Liberty, as personal life, is an inevitable assumption. It matters nothing that we find so much difficulty in its reconciliation with a divine government, or with the movement of the world. Liberty still remains the solvent of all intellectual activity. A man may refuse to recognize this inner law of rational life; he may leave the stream of human experience and sit upon the bank; but he cannot explain how he has gotten thus far save by a renewed recognition of the sufficiency of reason unto itself; nor can he, on any other terms, go any farther.

What has evolution to do with this perpetual paradox of life which is equally involved in science and religion—this point of contact between causes and reasons, between physical and spiritual movements? In the first place, it accepts in the most undeniable way the fact of contact, the presence of two irreducible terms equally essential to our knowledge. We will not return to our initiatory assertion of innumerable increments and omnipresent guidance, we simply draw attention to the many and marvellous ways in which man shapes to his own uses the lives with which his life is associated. Flowers, fruits; plants, trees; animals, great and small,—are tractable in his hand, and take on new forms at his bidding. He, of his own impulse, for his own ends, gives new conditions to vital forces; and they respond with marvellous quickness in new products, fitted to his physical service and to his intellectual tastes.

If there were an undeniable miracle which we could repeat as often as we chose, it could give no more proof of a supernatural presence than do these facts, which we renew at our pleasure, of man's true power over nature. The conclusion is involved in a universal and ever-growing experience. It is the one fact which we all love, in moments of philosophical acquiescence, to magnify—man's victories over the world.

Not only does evolution include these growing instances of man's potency, it allows the theoretical difficulties in the doctrine of liberty to fall into the background, where they keep company with a thousand things equally inconceivable with themselves. Evolution yields coherent phenomena, but leaves the ultimate grounds and terms of order to reason alone. It exposes no forces, it uncovers no causes, it declares no relations, it reveals no powers: it simply renders the sensuous terms of experience, and remits to the intellect of man their rational interpretation. It distinctly articulates its words, and requires us to understand them. He that hath ears to hear, let him hear. We are therefore in no way bound over to physical forces alone. We are left to render rational phenomena under rational terms as freely as material phenomena under material terms. Our notion of liberty is no more obscure, no less ultimate, than our notion of causation ; and, precisely like that notion, it marshals an immense number of phenomena to which it alone can give order. Evolution thus leaves us with the surface of the stream and the depths of the stream ; its smooth stretches, its ripples, its torn and angry surges—all alike suggestive.

Spiritual Phases of Evolution.

Phenomena are the provocations of reason, a perpetual appeal to the soul of man; the electric currents which we can in no way figure to the senses, but into whose intricate interplay we are diligently inquiring.

Evolution goes further. It shows the world to be vital as one whole. Reason is ever flowing into it and flowing out of it. It is as inevitably inductive of rational processes, and as certainly comes under their reaction, as one magnetic current affects by its immediate presence another. There are no laws which harass liberty, many laws which facilitate it; no decrees which bar freedom, many which demand its prompt use. There are no forces so self-contained that they do not stand on terms of relation with other forces. Make the material world as firm and inclusive as you will, and still influences from beyond it creep in upon it. Assert what you please of the spirituality of spiritual things, sensuous forces are constantly finding their way among them. These comings and goings we see, whether we know or do not know whence they come and whither they go. It is so on the supposition we have accepted in reference to divine agencies; it is so in reference to man as a spiritual being on any tenable theory concerning him. The physical does yield, constantly and freely yield, to the intellectual; is living stuff played upon by spiritual powers.

Under this conception, the embarrassment of decrees partially disappears. The time element is no longer troublesome. God is determining, not has determined, events. The mind and heart of God are here and now in the world, and give us the best possible opportunity to work with them in a living, loving, flexible way. So it is also, in our own action, if we bring man face to face with physical laws. They lose much of their fatalistic character. They do not preclude, they provoke, intervention. They make way for liberty. They are the servants of liberty. They have just that permanence and power which enable them to accept and store for us our activities. They have that well-defined response under them which reveals to us the methods of success. They are like well-tempered clay, which yields itself with sympathetic facility to the creative touch.

It is in the presence of an evolutionary world that we apprehend those sweeping words of our Lord: "Ask, and it shall be given you; seek, and ye shall find; knock, and it shall be opened unto you." The asking temper—a temper which expresses the steady momentum of the mind in the pursuit of its purposes—must prevail. All things flow together freely—from within and from without, from above and from below, from nature, from man and from God, in evolution. We stand centre-wise in creation : we create, and we are created. The ocean buoys us up, the winds blow for us; but we choose our guiding star, and our hand is on the helm. Are we not correct, then, in saying that evolution casts the clearest light we have on the most fundamental problem in personal life, the interaction of physical and spiritual things; more than this, that it reveals most certainly, and teaches most clearly, the growth and the method of growth by which the spiritual separates itself from the physical, and increasingly rules over it. Thus are the waters which are under the firmament divided from the waters which are above the firmament, yet with an habitual interplay ever more visible and more beneficent. The sense of a divine providence in our lives has been a ruling force in faith, yet it has brought with it endless confusion. If this providence has been regarded as strictly general, it has lost consolatory power. If it has been made special, it has failed in proof, and has readily become ridiculous. An evolution which constantly encloses us in the creative process, physical and spiritual, renders that providence at once comprehensive and pliant.

The steps which lead up to this more vital conception are themselves evolutionary. Man first comes to a sense of his own powers, exaggerates them, and gives them, in the interpretation of the world, wide inferential extension. Extreme as may be this separation of the personal element before the proper correction is present, it lies none the less in the direction of growth. Men come to recognize spiritual influences, and are made wakeful to them.

Later, men gain more knowledge of the physical world: they recognize its immense momentum, and the consequent limitations it brings to the will of man. This conception, in turn, becomes extreme, but, taken with the previous one, is corrective and constructive. Not till the two coalesce, and mutually qualify each other, does the world offer itself as at once truly physical and truly spiritual; not by division and by parts, but by interpenetration everywhere. The world is at any moment a definite and wholly intelligible product, but at every moment it is ready to take on higher and wider expression.

Thus we are led to substitute for "conversion," a sudden convulsive change in the spirit itself, growth, a slow healthy accumulation of life. We come to understand that our lives gain their true powers, not by being uprooted, but by being rooted in a more wholesome and comprehensive way in the world. We have made the same mistake in theology that we have made in penology. We have expected that a few concentrated and terrible motives would sweep from the heart of man its evil passions, and make it fruitful in obedience. We have not understood how many, how slight, how far and near, are the incentives which promote and secure spiritual development; and how confluent they must become from all quarters of the physical and social world before they can show their divine interlock and adequacy. A sudden surging-in of forces is no more conducive of spiritual growth than is a deluge of vegetable life. The dewdrops, the gentle, discontinuous rain, are the servants of God. The violent converging forces which express themselves in "conversion" are very inferior in productive power to the manifold, ever-varied, and ever-renewed incentives which steal in upon us from a world deeply at one with us in its wants and discipline. Indeed, to understand this concurrence of the outer and inner world is spiritual life. That development which gathers up the power of the world in our lives, and spreads our lives responsively over the world, is the only wide and growing union of the soul with God.

This evolution reconciles authority and reason. It may be true that nine tenths of our actions and our beliefs rest on authority; that ninety-nine hundredths of the efforts of men, and those the most successful, repose on custom. The supreme authority of reason is in no way weakened thereby. Seeds have not much bulk, but the potentialities of the world are in them. The buds of a tree are but a small portion of its entire mass, yet they alone are the significant parts. All has been built up in due order by them. The thoughts of men, as swayed by reason and reconstructed under it, are the intellectually vital points in the spiritual world. Here it is that human life takes on new forms, new powers, new promise. Reason leaves behind it a great deal of authority,—as the succulent bud deposits woody fibre—but no authority goes before it. Evolution is always directing our attention to the next significant change; and that is sure to be, in the spiritual world, the fresh product of thought. Authority does not enter in suspension of reason, it enters in enforcement of it. It checks inquiry which is superficial, inadequate, and captious. It presses the too loose earth around the roots, that these may take hold by contact and grow. Legitimate authority is only the emphasis to which sound reason is entitled. It is asserting ownership till a better right is offered. It is the lead of mind among minds that must be led.

So also the natural and the supernatural, with neither of which we have found ourselves able to dispense, are reconciled in evolution.

The natural absorbs the supernatural and becomes vital under it, as the dry, harsh sponge drinks in water and is instantly pliable in service; as the plant, awakening to new life in the springtime, puts forth power in all the strange, beautiful ways of its kind. A simply natural world, one finished to its last feature, exhausted of all further possibilities, is a dead world, is not at all the world of evolution. By the conception and by the fact of evolution we are in the midst of a creative process that moves so orderly that we can understand it, so slowly that we can take part in it, and with such growing significance that we feel at once its inspiration. Its supersensuous, supernatural force is disclosed in the marvellous increments it takes on; in the ruling idea nestled at its centre; in the care with which man, its most conspicuous intellectual product and concurrent agent, weaves his thought into it. We win, by a cordial recognition of the natural, not only a new world, but one of far greater breadth for the uses of the spirit than the one we left behind. Our powers take root at once by means of it; and what at first we seemed to lose, as a farmer loses the seed he sows, we quickly gain again, as the farmer gains his harvest. The fatal facility of our religious volitionalism, by which our will or the will of God is hardly more productive of permanent results than is the veering of the wind, disappears, and we find ourselves called on to incorporate our lives slowly, but forever, into the very substance of the creative process. All that the spirit of man has struggled for, and laid hold of in such an inadequate way in the supernatural,—a spiritual presence in the world, ready to put forth its strength in behalf of a divine order—is more than secured, it is translated into God immanent in the very heart of the world. The two spheres, physical and spiritual, are once more commensurate, once more melt into each other, as the mind into the body, and the body into the mind. Evolution thus exalts our personal potency to its highest terms, placing it in full possession of a world increasingly worth the possession. The natural is for the supernatural, the supernatural is by and through the natural.

There are many striking illustrations of the deeper meaning given to doctrines of faith by the theory of evolution. In place of the fall of Adam, original sin, inherited sin, the transmission of penalty to the third and fourth generation, we have the burden of an inferior animal life, only slowly shaken off, and permeated with utmost difficulty with higher, more vital impulses. The first series of beliefs is a rendering of the facts of human life theoretically, with inadequate knowledge; the second is a re-rendering of them, to the same ends, under an extended historical grasp of the situation. One is as much struck with the concurrence of the earlier and later doctrines as with their difference. Especially is this true in reference to their moral, disciplinary force. What a pathetic truthfulness is imparted to the experience of St. Paul: " I see another law in my members warring against the law of the mind, and bringing me into captivity to the law which is in my members. O wretched man that I am! Who shall deliver me from the body of this death?" The higher spiritual life has not yet won the government of the lower physical life. The inferior animal impulse thrusts itself forward constantly in limitation or in rejection of the superior intellectual one.

II.

Great as is the force of the evolutionary idea when taken in connection with our individual life, it is greater still in its disclosure of the true nature of our collective life. Whatever we may think about a rapid expansion of personal power, we are compelled to see that no such expansion is open to our communal strength, and that this strength must set limits to all the spiritual life associated with it. The flight of the bird must be measured by the extent of the atmosphere in which it moves. It belongs to genius to somewhat transcend customary boundaries: it does not belong to it to transcend them in all degrees. The stroke of its wing must bring some reaction to it, or it soon fails.

We indicate a few of the ways in which our collective life finds expansion and consolidation by evolution—a separation of parts, and a gathering together of parts in a more truly organic form. Our religious life—the construction of a supersensuous experience in wise and beneficent response to our sensuous experience—is plainly one of social development. It calls, like fine art, for a penetrative, subtile, ever-renewed insight into the inner force of those physical and social facts which we are weaving together in history. Men go stumbling on in the religious world, as those whose vision has not yet been adjusted to the attenuated light about them. Our religious ideas need, above all other ideas, to be empirically correct, to conform to an experience which has grown up with them and supports them. It is difficult, with a difficulty greater than we encounter in any other direction, to bring to them this constant reconstruction, this growing response to the social world. Our religious ideas are rarely our own. Somebody has us by the hand, and we have somebody by the hand. We move forward in awkward squads, thinking ourselves not lost in the darkness merely because there are so many of us. Contact with other moving masses becomes collision, and none of us quite gain our eyes or win our feet. Our religious experience is so vague, so variable and conventional, so much aside from the daily conditions of life, that we meet with the greatest difficulty in making it sober, coherent, and progressive. We have yet to develop spiritual organs thoroughly fitted to their work, and to acquire ease in the use of them.

Hitherto, far from collating the religious history of the world, we have flung aside all but our own portion of it, and have assigned that an absolute character which has robbed it of much of its instruction. To secure cosmic terms in faith—and here, even more than elsewhere, the widest is the truest rendering—is the tardy result of a most perplexing and painful experience, one vibrating between unreasonable fear and unreasonable hope, between belief and unbelief, alike extreme. Men have held their religious dogmas aloof from the world, and have paid little or no attention to the most obvious contradictions between the two. They have overborne the spiritual facts of the world by a preconception concerning them. It has been far from their thoughts to make the revelation they received the counterpart of man's development. Yet religious ideas that do not receive this correction become fantastic and visionary beyond all other ideas. Nowhere is the cleansing, evolutionary flow more necessary, if we are to reach in our thoughts, so quickly driven forward by fanaticism, so easily stagnant in superstition, so readily directed by dogmas, anything like transparency, purity, and liberty. It is only by many collidings, a long churning of our religious ideas together, that we can come, even proximately, to undertand their worth and their want of worth, and to share the higher life which is being developed into vision by virtue of changes organically wrought here and there through the whole range of human experience.

A second form of growth with which we meet with difficulty only a little less embarrassing is that of ethical law. This law lies chiefly, and always most clearly, between man and man. The multiplying relations of life, continually gaining greater breadth and greater depth, must be measured on the surface with more accuracy, and plumbed to the bottom with truer feeling, if we are to grasp their constructive, their ethical law. The moral order of the world is the supreme order, and we cannot attain to it save as the result of the largest experience and the most comprehensive insight. The very fact of our disobedience to the law hides the law from us, and serves to confuse it in its practical development. Thoroughly as we may believe that this last analysis of a physico-spiritual world into ethical law is germane to human reason, we shall be compelled to see that it can complete itself only under the most varied and protracted experience—one that opens up somewhere, at some time, in some person, or some nation, all the possibilities of conduct and character; nay, more than this, that works them into a social life so translucent with truth that it cannot again confound itself. So we win an ethical reason instructed by the revelation of the world. The comprehending thought and the comprehended facts run parallel to each other, and call out growth between them, as a fertile soil and a genial climate receive to themselves the germs of life that lie trembling on the limits of a new species.

These two things, ethical law and spiritual life, must fully affiliate before either can complete itself. Both must find extended presentation in the masses of men. The centre of gravity in the spiritual world lies deep beneath the surface. Our spiritual impulses can gain volume and extension only as they prevail over a wide area. Inertia and momentum alike— the power to resist, and the power to impel— are due to the magnitude of the world. Its superficial magnetic currents stand connected with its inner magnetic force. Separation in the spiritual world is fatal to energy.

The moral law is the intellectual side of our higher life, its framework of order, its theoretical harmony and completeness. Religious faith is the vital, emotional side of this life, is the sensitive flesh which clothes the skeleton of law, is an overflowing sense of the joy and excellency of that which the law embraces and defines.

These two, which come together like correct

outline and warm color in art, arise none the less somewhat separately in human experience, and are only slowly united; the surface of adequate and lasting union being the popular life, the tissue of our social state.

Moral law, as a detached experience, found remarkable expression in the Stoics, and yet showed little power in correcting the very great social evils with which it was in contact. Stoicism affiliated with the nobler phases of Roman character, and that when moral and civic degeneration had set in in an irresistible tide. It was united, as a philosophy of life, with impurity in the household, arbitrary authority in the state, the exactions of luxury by the few, impudent beggary by the populace, and a cruelty in all which made of human suffering, as presented in the amphitheatre, a passionate public amusement. The true intellectual insight of Stoicism is seen in the fact that it was the product of a few superior minds; was the same whether developed in the experience of a slave, like Epictetus, or in that of an Emperor, like Marcus Aurelius Antoninus; and that it at no time became a popular possession. Vice surged about it wholly unaffected.

Though the ethical excellence of Stoicism failed to become a ruling force in social life, it was not lost in the great aggregate of human experience. Civil law has always been the most adequate and continuous expression, in the general life, of ethical principles. Much as it may at many points fall below them, it is ever attracted to them, and shows a partial parallelism with them. Roman law, a product in justice and breadth much beyond the social life with which it was associated, owed much to the ethics of Stoicism, and has helped, in the descent of legal principles in England and on the Continent, to give to the general mind, in a large class of transactions, notions of equity from which it will not again depart. While Stoicism was not able to spread over the popular mind and possess it, it became a fountain to the narrow stream of civil law that has kept company with the race in desolate periods and places.

Religious development in its highest phase, that of Christianity, separated itself somewhat positively from morality. It neither apprehended truth as truth and loved it as truth, nor life as life and rejoiced in it as life. The ethical law is the law of life, both in its present form and in its later developments. It offers most subtile and variable phases of truth, and must be searched for with that sensitive, penetrating, and earnest temper which is able to reconcile the possibilities of the present with the hopes of the future. The religious development of the third century and the centuries following was not indifferent to the truth, but so utterly misconceived it as to become, in its bigotry and exaction, a most dangerous enemy to it. It virtually arrested the growth of ethical law by checking that personal inquiry and freedom of action which are its essence. Down to our own time, religious faith has been more or less conscious of this antagonism, and has not infrequently attacked morality as a wholly inadequate law of life, and in opposition to faith.

Religious belief for a long time, by asceticism, celibacy, monasticism, opposed itself to life, mutilated and macerated it, impoverished and imbittered it, despised and humbled it. The world, the flesh, and the devil became, in religious thought, the trinity of evil against which an exterminating warfare was to be waged. The mere shadow of truth which there was in these conceptions did not suffice to correct the deep antagonism they involved to ethical law, to a life to be redeemed in itself under its own best impulses. Spiritual incentives were framed and enforced, long and wide, in painful detachment from those large claims which our personal powers and social relations make upon us. Religion narrowed the thoughts, and gave the affections a wholly inadequate field. Instead of making the world the Kingdom of Heaven, it waited with impatience for a purification by fire. Its millennium was one of convulsion and overthrow.

The religious life, as more emotional and less intellectual, as more conventional and less personal, took more ready possession of the popular mind than did the severe and grand conceptions of ethical insight. Many have been at a loss to understand why the Stoics so signally failed to apprehend Christianity, and found in it repulsion rather than attraction. The superficial, yet most obvious, collision of Christianity with that large, personal life which was the ideal of Stoicism, sufficiently explains this alienation. How could the two coalesce, when they held in such a divisive way the two great elements in spiritual life—the integrity of its inner law, on the one side; and the affections, on the other? These experiences, in the form in which they were most urgently offered, were to the Stoic degrading superstitions; and the wealth of its supersensuous promises and those ethical injunctions which filled the mind of the Stoic with a sense of supreme order, were to the Christian cold, powerless abstractions, quite as likely to lead those who dwelt on them away from life, as into life. A conflict allied to this everywhere attends on development—a rush for the amenities and rewards of faith, with no adequate sense of its inner scope and power; or something of this deeper vision united to an indisposition to reproduce it in the lives of men.

Does not the "secret of Christ"—whosoever will save his life shall lose it, and whosoever shall lose his life for my sake and the gospel's, the same shall save it—lie in the line of reconciliation? The Stoic took the ethical law in its breadth and grandeur, but without that immediate sense of a divine presence and those universal affections which make obedience easy and rewardful. The Christian struggled for the supersensuous impressions; but not grounding them in ethical law, in human experience, they became fanciful, extravagant, and without permanent productive power. Is it not true that the scope of our lives is so great on the one side, and the immediate social contradictions to them so many on the other side, that they necessarily present an appearance of hopeless conflict? The Christian escapes this confusion in part by a violent spiritual uplift, which struggles to make for itself an independent centre. The Stoic—and the doctrine is always with us in noble natures—fills his mind with a fine sense of ethical law, and then defies the events which are constantly assailing his defences. Each strives to win a life beyond the life about them, the one in an emotional, the other in an intellectual, region. Christ bids us lose our lives, the immediate joy and comfort of them, in a universal struggle for the true conditions of life, and to win back a masterful life, carrying its own conquering impulses into our hourly experiences. We are to plant, cultivate, and ripen our virtues in the sterile soil and under the harsh climate which enclose us, till there comes to be a spiritual fertility begotten out of the corrected processes of culture itself. We conquer by submission, but we conquer. This is profoundly rational, but it is also profoundly evolutionary. The actual and the ideal are made to work together in all that is good. What is yielded is yielded in reference to winning it back again in a better form. There is no defiance and no contempt; no casting away of anything that is good, but a working with it upward into a more comprehensive good.

Some, as Mr. Kidd in his *Social Evolution*, have recognized the power of religious faith in developing wide altruistic impulses which were to harmonize society and reconcile its conflicting classes; but they have regarded this movement as a supernatural one, or, with Mr. Kidd, as extra rational. This view hides from us the ethical law, the law of reason, profoundly implanted in the very nature of man. Order, under this conception, is induced from without, not gained from within by growth. There is no end of conflict between impulse and impulse, man and man, class and class, in short periods and near relations; extend the period, broaden the spaces, enrich the spirit, give life its true circumference, and the larger evolutionary law makes its appearance. Men coalesce by virtue of a superior habit of thought. An altruism induced as an irrational habit on a spiritual nature alien to it, could never become the ground of permanent order. The inner conflict, uncorrected, would fret against the restraints put upon it, and might at any moment break out afresh. The spiritual development, when it comes, must be supremely natural.

The altruistic elements in our physical nature and surroundings are truly altruistic, our power a collective power. As certainly also are the deeper impulses in our intellectual and in our social constitution altruistic. Our thoughts grow wise, clear, and strong under extended personal impact; our affections are gladdened by sympathy, and this altruism goes on to complete itself in the law of love. That law sends fibres into the lowest subsoil of our physical and economic prosperity, draws nourishment from it, and returns to it a fresh fertility, incident to its own higher growth. The hope and courage of our time are especially found in a new interpretation of all interests, a reconciliation of all lines of development. Our religious faith is submitting itself to the correction of ethical ideas, is taking up the precise duties assigned it in society, and is carrying love and law into its own life and the popular life. Our highest beliefs are becoming empirical, and our nearest experiences are receiving the leaven of spiritual truth. Thus are the terms on either side, which make up the Kingdom of Heaven, united. The real is idealized, and the ideal is realized. The law of love is tested and confirmed by a comprehensive and complex life subject to it, and that life is disclosed in its inner law by means of it. Unless the work of God and the word of God coalesce in a fulfilment of this order, there can be no victory for either of them. Evolution is bringing together the inner force and the outer form, the integrity of truth and the inspiration of truth, making by the two a new disclosure of the divine mind.

III.

We need to define evolution anew, if we are to see clearly the precise way in which events are being knit together. While the conception of evolution we accept is thoroughly theistic, stated simply on the formal side, it does not differ very much from purely mechanical evolution. Evolution involves an empirical unfolding of human life as opposed to a volitional one. Both experience and instruction, the necessities of the case perceived by ourselves and the coercion of a superior will, enter into our daily lives. It is a difficult problem in discipline, in the nurture of children, in the training of young men, in the government of the state, to reconcile these two terms. Some strive to reach the desired result of good order off hand, by constraint. The child is made momentarily to feel authority, the young man is met at every turn by a rigid regulation, the criminal is pursued by a relentless punishment. This volitional discipline is the first tendency, the crude thought, among men; but its results have never been satisfactory. It fails to correct ignorance or evoke good-will, and often leaves the mind in a blind and perverse mood. Hence a more slowly corrective, a more nutritive, system is coming to take its place. The discipline is made empirical. The mind is quickened by its own processes; the events of life are made to interpret and enforce themselves, and to yield to the awakened feelings the motives to virtue which they really contain. There is something of the same difference between a volitional impression and an empirical lesson that there is between a device painted on the arm and one pricked into the flesh, between a remedy that for the moment checks disordered action in the physical system and one which steadily re-restores it to its normal state.

The doctrine of evolution regards the discipline of the world as thoroughly empirical. The mind is taught and strengthened by its own rendering of events, and by the response of events to it. Erroneous and evil impulses are displaced by those wiser and more salutary. We have great difficulty, while accepting in a general way this government of the world by growth, in recognizing fully what it involves. It sets aside optimism, except that optimism which is contained in the very fact of a scheme of development as opposed to one of overruling counsel. Optimism includes at every step the recognition of some method, some form of action, as the very best, and its instant introduction. It finds no difficulty in doing and in having the best. The best is clearly defined for it. Its feeling is allied to that of the father who proposes to carry his son smoothly along a prosperous path by the pressure and bestowments of his own right hand. This optimism, this volitional method, is inconsistent with itself. It unites incompatible elements. Strength, virtue, while they are recognized as the products of will in one's own life, are made the products of a foreign will in another's life. While the spiritual state must be personal, if, when it has been won, it is to be of any value, the winning of it is largely by an exterior, impersonal process. The volitional element easily destroys its own significance, after it has entered our experience, by this undue extension of it.

Voluntaryism is no more admissible as a divine method of remedying the evils of the world. If volition can do any and every thing, it can undo any and every thing, and nothing is truly done. Voluntary effort preserves its value by being firmly inwrought with that which is not voluntary, but is an aggregate of the everlasting forces and laws of the world. It is thus we secure creation. We cannot even take part in a game,—as that of chess—if we insist on replacing our men to suit an exigency, or on varying the rules of play to meet an immediate want. The will measures itself and preserves itself along the fixed lines of causation. It is these that present the wise problem of wise over sight, and these that hold fast each of the terms in its solution.

The discipline of the world on its physical side is, and may well be, more purely empirical, because it is associated with nurture,—counsel and aid among men—and is thereby supplemented and strengthened on the personal side. Persuasion, command, freedom, come with persons, and make the basis of stern necessity and inflexible law in things the more apparent and the more necessary. We should be building on quicksand, if all were volitional. We often suffer, as it is, by putting another's knowledge in place of our own knowledge, another's will for our own will. The personal element in the government of the world comes to us chiefly through the persons in the world, and by its nearness to our lives, its warmth of affection, its evident potency over events, prevents our conceiving the world as a dead piece of mechanism. We are helped toward the vital conception—a conception so natural, so inevitable, yet one which so many have found beset with contradictions—of the world as something being made, holding in itself each moment a changing possibility, an eternal potency. We are not allowed to fall into an insect sort of logic, that spins its entire thread from one centre, and makes its conclusions the grave of its powers.

The empirical discipline of the world is constantly misapprehended even by those who accept it. It does not allow of any criticism of the divine movement as too slow and too painful. Such fault-finding implies that a stroke of will, a little outside pressure or compulsion, could overcome this evil, and quicken development. It is as in training one of a feeble mind. The effort must be cautious, patient, never at a pace that overmasters the powers. Any pushing of the thoughts confuses them, entangles them afresh. Any urgency of love repels the feeble affections. The plant is "drawn," not strengthened, by a strong light in a single direction. So able and candid a critic as Lecky speaks in this way: "The period of Catholic ascendency was, on the whole, one of the most deplorable in the history of the human mind. The energies of Christendom were diverted from all useful and progressive studies, and were wholly expended on theological disquisitions." *—" Mediæval Catholicism discouraged and suppressed in every way secular studies, while it conferred a monopoly of wealth, and honour, and power upon the distinguished theologians." † While

---

* *History of European Morals.* W. E. H. Lecky, vol. ii., p. 218.
† *Ibid.*, p. 222.

this language is very intelligible and very truthful as the expression of a feeling which belongs to a later and a higher position, it contains an implication quite at war with a correct conception of evolution. The scientist tells us what religion has done and failed to do, and the religionist responds with his censures of science in its spiritual impulses. But there is neither religion nor science as an entity working any results, good or bad, in human history. The method of expression is a convenient one by which we refer this and that result to religion or to science, and we do not hesitate, therefore, to use it; but it is wholly a figurative one, and may readily be very misleading. There are at any one time such and such men, with certain predilections, with an experience of lights and shadows of a given kind. All that is possible to the race at any one place and time, is an unfolding of the dominant phase of life, a pushing of it forward into the successes and failures normal to it, and so making ready for a later separation and relation as experience shall pronounce upon them. The theologian has not, with far-sighted perversity, anticipated and forestalled scientific inquiry. He has not diverted energies which were ready for useful studies from their pursuit. He has simply obeyed the dominant impulse as he and others conceived it. He has given life the expansion it was seeking.

When the scientific tendency arose, it had its own personal life, gained its extension in a reactionary way from a previous period, and fell at once under its own limitations. We are only waiting for a higher altitude to condemn, in a very unqualified way, the secular, unspiritual impulses which arise in connection with physical inquiries too zealously and too exclusively pursued. The sphere of personal liberty and personal responsibility is a great deal narrower than this language, so familiar to us, implies. The correction follows after, and is involved in, the error, and itself gives rise to a new error and a further correction. We spiritualize and we secularize our notions in succession as a slow and painful method of bringing the two elements together, yet the movement can by no possibility be made greatly different from what it is. We take each his own part in it, make our mistakes, and encounter our responsibilities; but the germinant, volitional cell, significant as it always must be, revolves under a swirl of events much too powerful for it.

It is convenient for us to speak as if we got in each other's way,—and in a very limited measure we do—but the assertion does not, under evolution, express any fundamental fact. It is simply projecting a narrow volitional outlook of our own on the world at large. Error and correction, religion and science, are equally included in evolution. The error seems to delay us; yet it compels the correction, and gives to our thoughts a clearness not otherwise attainable. The obstinacy of faith makes inquiry the more bold, and the baldness of the physical statement drives us back again to the inner rendering of the mind.

The intellectual and volitional experiences which play around this movement are transient and relatively trifling. Much as they may contain of our individual wealth, they do not measure our collective wealth. They are at no time controlling. They are at best a photosphere—an exterior glory which rests back on a permanent productive centre. The theologian is as certainly after his kind as is the scientist after his kind. Each has a weighty part in the great aggregate of life. There comes, in reference to each, a moment of selection, in which they give way to something beyond themselves, but their own offspring. The theologian now experiences the disadvantage of having overlived his hour, and the scientist the advantage of entering on his hour. The distinction is not material. As in the parable of the servants hired into the vineyard, the reward may be much the same, though the hours of starting work are diverse. The growing integrity of life in all its forms is what we need to see, and to make its consolation irrevocably our own under this supreme idea of evolution. Each phase of human experience stands in a productive relation, backward and forward, and, having exhausted its ministrations, gives way to a more immediately effective form. Evolution is not pledged to make no mistakes, to occasion no delays. Quite the reverse. Every marked achievement is simply a departure from things defective in reference to it; each superior form of life gains ground by contrast. All that the conception involves, is that a generative and shifting process shall go forward, and that it will issue in a progress of the most undeniable and permanent character. The growth achieved will take possession of the soil beneath and the air above, and unite them in new and productive ways; will, like a plant, inhale the atmosphere of the world, and cast its own spores into that atmosphere. Yet, tardy as this movement, looked on collectively, may seem to be, no one ever takes part in it, pursues it in the form of truth, or crystallizes it in the form of character, and finds himself straitened in his opportunities and resources. The victory that comes to him he owes as much to difficulties as to facilities, to ways that he has opened for himself as to ways that have been opened for him.

The generative processes are more rapid in the intellectual and the spiritual world than in the physical world, and the selection more comprehensive and positive. There is physical selection of physical strength, and intellectual selection of truth; ethical selection of righteousness, and æsthetical selection of beauty; social selection of organic force, and spiritual selection of divine inspiration. All concur, and, though their full concurrence calls for a wide empirical life, there are also correspondingly numerous affinities that are pushing for it in many invincible ways. Though physical evolution seems the slowest, most independent, and most difficult portion of this conjoint development, as a matter of fact, we find it to-day in advance rather than in rear of the general movement. The powers which men are coming to have at their disposal, as in the case of fire-arms and dynamite, are in excess of the moral temper they are bringing to their use. If social progress were proportioned to physical progress, physical progress would receive at once a marvellous impulse. The facility of thought, if it can be made to issue on the one side in spiritual evolution, is sure to issue on the other in an astonishing mastery of the world. The real drag is in the moral temper, and the delay tends to correct and instruct that temper. It is evolution as an empirical discipline, a steady comminuting and commingling of the elements of life, that we wish to consider in a few of its spiritual phases.

If we accept evolution as a truly rational theory of the universe; if we see no other way in which life and knowledge, freedom and power, can be made so wide, so universal, so substantial a possession, then the slowness of the movement is inseparable from its nature, and ceases to be an objection. As in the building-up of a Japanese vase, the only question that remains pertinent is, Does the beauty of the product justify the labor? The movement is sure to be as rapid as it can be, all its liabilities, its misdirections and redirections, being duly weighed. They all play their part in the final product. The only points of haste and urgency are those personal, volitional ones where we ourselves act on the process, and are acted on by it. It is here that the sense of great need and great power germinates in a higher life. As in the flow of the glaciers, it is here that the immense pressure dissolves and then reunites the molecules.

The same is true in reference to suffering. We have only one simple question to answer: Are intellectual life and spiritual life worth the winning? This being conceded, it is no longer rational for us to bewail each new hardship. The suffering of the world is an inseparable part of its discipline. It is the disclosure of failure, complete or partial. It corrects our errors, gives tone to our social life, and is the background of our spiritual joys. Suffering is an essential element in human experience, rendered in terms of evolution, and, like delay, is measured by the very exigency in which it is involved. The suffering is the exigency, and the exigency is the suffering.

The question is not, whether life is worth living, looked on as a present aggregate of pains and pleasures, of woes and joys, but whether an adequate goal of so mixed an experience is before us? The world, once redeemed into its own proper life, would push the query aside as of no force. A woman, when she is in travail, hath sorrow because her hour is come; but so soon as she is delivered of the child, she remembereth no more the anguish for joy that a man is born into the world.

The suffering in animal life we believe to be greatly exaggerated, and, such as it is, to be an inseparable subordinate part that goes with the entire scheme. It is a victory over death that we are winning; and that not for ourselves only, but for the whole creation, that travaileth in pain until now. We do not labor these points. They are all involved in evolution, and we accept evolution both as a fact and as a scheme. Life rejoices in itself; and the higher the life, the greater the joy. Grief, despondency, are simply the decadence of life, the retardation of the movement, grinding upon itself. Movement, evolution, is a universal joy, "a joy forever." We are waiting only for a confluence of forces, a harmony of sweet sounds, the instant when creation discloses itself to itself.

The fundamental points in this doctrine of development, as associated with religious life, are, whether evolution is truly applicable to that life; whether the phases of spiritual experience through which we are passing do correct each other, and lead to a general uplift of thought and action; and whether the mind can accept growth as an ultimate result.

Is there a spiritual life—a life of its own order, the natural continuation and fulfilment of the life we now lead? Comparatively few have failed to catch sight, less or more clearly, of this promise of the future, but have found it opposed, in the forms in which it has been offered, to the nature of man and the facts of the world. It has frequently been accepted in flat contradiction of existing things, and frequently been denied because no such contradiction was a tenable belief. Evolution not only requires an ever more complete life, but that this life should be thoroughly integrated with, and the product of, our present life. Animality, rationality, spirituality, are not only ascending terms in one movement: they are sustaining and completing terms as well. Evolution is not allied to motion, which, in assuming a new position, forsakes the old one, but to growth, which includes with what it gains all that has already been acquired.

By spirituality we understand the presence in the mind, as constant incentives of thought and action, as interpreting and exhilerating conceptions, of those supersensuous relations which unite us to an invisible world, and are its framework. Religious faith gives these ideas in their most ample and effective form. That these conceptions multiply and become more forceful as men progress in knowledge, is simply a fact of history. Scepticism and agnosticism of all kinds, which arise in contention with these ideas and in reduction of their powers, serve only to correct and extend them; never, to any great degree or for any long period, to uproot them. The certainty with which every phase of unbelief becomes ultimately a foil in the training-school of belief, and so passes away, is a most significant fact in spiritual philosophy. That men push forward, under the influence of spiritual ideas, and develop in turn these ideas, as they advance, is as universal an induction as any associated with human history. Over against it is the correlative law that races decay in the measure in which they drop off from super-sensuous conceptions, and become sensuous in their lives. The sensuous life cannot be maintained at any high level of comfort divorced from the spiritual life. In other words, there is an insatiable religious impulse, hidden in the human mind, which is sure to find development, and to become a ruling element in physical and social experiences. The fact, then, of growth in a spiritual direction, is a most obvious and significant one as rendered in the life of the race.

Not much less plain is the second fact, that this higher life in no way divorces itself from the lower life from which it springs, but takes it up into itself. This is seen in the ruling, empirical tendency which has overtaken our knowledge. The speculation of the past, detaching itself from experience, became barren. Men turned back in weariness to things, events, history, and immediately thought became fruitful again. Theory, rooting itself in the soil, grew sturdily in the air, and the several forms of intellectual activity assumed toward each other nutritive relations.

The same is true in art, another direction in which supersensuous elements freely enter. A romantic or an ideal tendency soon exhausts itself, if it loses its governing conditions in physical things. It then gives place to a realism which contents itself with reproducing the phenomenal world. Still more quickly does this become barren unless it leads to a new evolution of inner life. The outer form and inner force must accompany each other at every step, or art becomes uninteresting and uninstructive. Its mastery is found in spiritual impulses expended on physical things—restraint and concession here, concession and coercion there.

The religious life has striven very pertinaciously and protractedly to divorce itself from the world—to leave behind it its physical and social terms, and many even of its intellectual conditions. It has signally failed. The significant features of our time are found in the degree in which faith is beginning to return upon itself, and take up anew its neglected duties; is learning to resuscitate and rehabilitate its life, making it healthy and rugged on the physical and social sides; to correct its thinking by the facts of the world, restoring fully its connection with them; and, above all, to develop its affections afresh, man with man, class with class, nation with nation, drawing all into the Kingdom of Heaven. Our experience is rendering itself in terms of evolution with advances, retreats, and alternations. Higher things are offered to us, but they can be attained only under conditions of life which we may easily and ignorantly suffer to become sordid. This truth receives many illustrations.

When the principles of economics began to disclose themselves, men felt that they had hit upon laws that needed only to be followed to secure general prosperity. Here were ultimate truths, and ultimate lines of conduct, that admitted of free and independent development. An experience, prosperous in its own narrow circle, far from showing the justness of this view, has led us forward into graver perplexities, more pervasive and difficult problems, than any hitherto encountered. Capital, instead of being harmoniously at work with labor, the two organized evermore completely into a common life, is accumulated in great amounts, and confronts, in an aggressive and hostile attitude, labor, also gathered in corresponding masses. The two, compelled to support each other, do it with reluctance and ill will. The need of more comprehensive, just, and generous impulses is universally felt. They must be had, or the whole movement is threatened with miscarriage and slow decay. A social life that embraces all, has its rewards for all, and carries the stimuli of contented activity to the lowest stratum of society, is a necessity of the common strength, and so, in long periods and over broad surfaces, of the individual strength. Social equilibrium is attainable only by organic force; and, till this is secured, there is and must be a restless casting about, on this side and on that, to attain or to retain a prosperity not provided for in the social facts themselves. Society cannot be built, in any portion of its interests, firmly and restfully on economic laws, save as these are united with ethical laws in mutual guidance and restraint. All the wants of men, as one complex adjustment, find satisfaction together. We cannot take up our social life piecemeal. Every gain brings new relations and new dispositions. The movement is strongly evolutionary, its steps successive and closely interdependent. Every satisfaction becomes a demand, and every demand an imperative impulse.

The same truth is equally apparent in civic action. It is easy to regard free government as a wide and universal remedy of misrule. As a matter of fact, it brings new dangers and imposes fresh duties. The problem of wise government is not escaped. It is carried over to the people who are but poorly instructed in it, and who are subject to many influences unfavorable to its solution. The perplexities of a free people are exceedingly comprehensive, are constantly returning, and accept correction only by many modifications over a wide area through long periods. The chief advantage of liberty lies in this persistent demand. Eternal vigilance is the price of liberty, not simply in anticipation of its overthrow, but as providing the conditions of its successful development. We cannot take a single step in the direction of freedom without being compelled thereby to take many more. Each new equilibrium calls for an extended re-adjustment of the social forces which take part in it ; and this the more, because every satisfied desire makes way for other desires which stand hidden behind it. The variability of social relations, and the variability of the principles applicable to them, are the most conspicuous facts in society.

No incentives are more mutually corrective, upward and downward, than spiritual ones. They all push forward to and converge in the coming of the Kingdom of Heaven. The petitions of the Lord's Prayer are so few because they are so comprehensive, and because, by this comprehensiveness, they lead us straight on through a thousand secondary desires that might bewilder and mislead us, and plant us at the centre of hope. It is better to go back from this centre to each separate necessity than to be embarrassed by it as we approach the centre itself. It is a sense of the Kingdom of Heaven that defines for us the conditions of life, and their true relation to each other.

But let this sense of a Kingdom be with us, and how rapidly it spreads over the entire social field, with a sharp decisive discrimination between actions! Nothing is untouched by it. The least as well as the largest interest is ruled under it into order. The Kingdom of Heaven is a physical, intellectual, social, and spiritual product. It adjusts all things and persons to each other. Like music, it cannot bear a discord anywhere, and therefore the spirit really open to this impulse is indifferent to nothing, is put in possession of the entire world for constructive, spiritual purposes.

A great many Christian men and all Christian nations quietly accept such a thing as war, but it is because they have not fully felt that central power of a higher life which is drawing them out of chaos into creation. When the creative impulse shall unfold itself a little farther, they will feel that poverty, passion, violence in every form and wherever present, are opposed to it; that war, in which men dash in pieces organic construction already achieved, and kindle fresh dissension, is most antithetic to that Kingdom—a visible break from under its gracious and growing processes. When the mind, in any good measure, becomes Christlike, and has cast upon it, as its own personal burden, the redemption of the world,—its physical poverty, its intellectual discord, its spiritual destitution—it will find itself in the midst of evolutionary forces of infinite variety, gaining, losing, contending in all ways in the struggle of life. It will be compelled to go over many times the barren spaces which religion has left behind it, and provide for all the virtues, all the enjoyments, all the varied impulses of manifold powers and rich experiences.

If we look broadly at human history, it is not an unsafe induction, nor one without great significance, that a satisfaction of wants among men opens up a wider and higher circle of wants ; and that these later and larger wants are also more harmonious between man and man, more controlling downward of the strife beneath them, more uplifting toward the circle which still lies above them. This means that a spiritual evolution embraces us whose direction we can discern, and whose several stages are gaining hold on our conscious, social life.

Spiritual evolution has its own forms of atavism. If a nation is brought into the field of a higher life, and turns back in luxury and debauch on a lower life ; if it strives to appropriate the gains of growth, not as conditions for farther growth, but for immediate, sensual pleasure, it loses its footing shortly, and sinks into a lower stage. Each advance gives occasion to new social claims which we must proceed to meet, or they involve us in dissension, weakness, and regression.

The essential features of evolution are present in the spiritual history of the world. Each succeeding stage is more comprehensive, more organic, than the previous one. The completion of each movement is in that which follows it. Every movement involves so delicate a poise of forces that it must pass on to a higher movement or it loses its own equilibrium and perishes. The law and the prophets must be fulfilled in something superior to themselves, or they squander their own wealth.

Under this conception, so full of light, yet a light so subtile and changeable that each man must catch for himself its flitting forms, we feel assured of the general spiritual trend of the world. We seem also to be able to discover the part which certain painful phases of spiritual life, offering themselves, first as great aims, then as obstacles, and later as failures, have really subserved. The development of Christian dogma presents an example suited to our purpose as a very distinguishable, emphatic, and painstaking form of effort, and one very familiar to us.

What we have to see, and what we need to show, under this conception of evolution is, that the doctrinal beliefs that have been current at any period have been normal to its intellectual and social condition, have been productive of progress, and, through the evils they have developed, have ultimately opened the way to more adequate statements. The lower belief has been a preparation for the higher belief, and, in the very resistance it has offered to it, has become a means to its more complete development and its more general acceptance. The spiritual growth has lain between the two, in their action and reaction on each other.

Take, as a first example, the doctrine of sin, with its doom of endless punishment. The belief assumed for many centuries a form truly appalling, and is now pushed aside by the thoughtful and sympathetic mind with strong moral revulsion. Yet it is perfectly plain that this dogma has played an important part in the development of society, and has helped it upward to its advanced ethical standing. The better opinion has been born of the inferior one, and, in legitimate descent, has replaced it. The education of man proceeds at no point more slowly than in attaining a proportionate and just estimate of all forms of offence. It is the life-long discipline of the individual, and the unending lesson of society. The schooling of civil and criminal law for many centuries has been this very thing—a better definition of injuries and a more adequate apprehension of penalties. Action can only become ethical—a method seen and enforced by the individual himself—as the mind is awakened by the most varied and protracted experience to all the bearings of conduct, and is made able to meet them with a complexity of thought equal to their own complexity.

The conscience is more easily awakened by the idea of sin, an offence committed against God, than by a violation of the moral law, action faulty in reference to one's self or one's neighbor. Indeed, down to our own time, the most intelligent men experience great difficulty in conceiving the true character of injuries inflicted on nations other than their own. The moral law suffers suspension in so remote a field. A sin against God, like an offence against a chief, in the earliest period easily alarmed the guilty spirit. The sinner had no difficulty in conceiving the bad consequences which were likely to follow from the sin. Hence in awakening and deepening the sense of wrongfulness, and of its correlative, rightfulness,—the sense on whose delicacy and justness all later training was to depend — this magnifying of sin, as a wrong directed against God,

Spiritual Phases of Evolution. 145

became a primary term. The sensitive conscience, for its own sake and for the sake of others, enhanced the consequences of sin. It secured by this means its reactionary spring towards obedience.

An essential step in this process was dwelling on punishment. In the early history of men, punishment is far more the measure of transgression than any insight into the offence itself. An injury to a superior, followed by a sudden and severe penalty, was well understood; an injury to an inferior, followed by no rebuke, was lightly thought of. As the punishment of sin was not obvious nor immediate, the mind, in the enhancement of trangression, made the penalty the greater and the more enduring, till the doctrines of eternal punishment and of purgatory were fully developed. It was first the moral training, and then the moral pressure, of these dogmas that led men to a deeper study of the entire problem.

Some have been led, very mistakenly, to regard these doctrines as priest-craft, devices conceived and kept alive for ends of personal control. Men are not so readily led as this rendering of events implies, nor are the leaders of men so much disposed to mislead them.

Leaders and led necessarily rest their intellectual construction of events on much the same basis. The conscious perversion of ideas for an ulterior object is very slight when compared with the great flow of moral forces in men's minds which makes this perversion possible. When leaders cease to believe what they teach, they will soon cease to inspire belief. Belief in the popular mind and in the priestly mind is essentially one. Like people, like priest; like priest, like people, are aphorisms thoroughly supported by experience. The restraints which attended in action on the preaching of the doctrine of future punishment was, to those who taught it, an additional evidence of its truth. President Edwards enforced the doctrine in a most unequivocal form, and that not simply in the presence of intelligence, but as the fruit of intelligence—as one factor in a consistent system of doctrine.

The belief was associated with other beliefs which helped to make it rational. God was not simply holy, he was the ruler of the world, and was involved in all the claims of justice. Not till the idea of justice had gained more adequate statement could that of beneficence find free entrance. The administration of the spiritual world was inextricably tangled up with all the embarrassments which beset human law. To launch out on ethical forces, acting by themselves and supreme, implied a boldness of thought far beyond the experience and habits of men's minds. Sin was measured not from its own centre, the mind and heart of the sinner, but from the centre of the spiritual universe; by its remoteness from the mind of God; by the injury it was thought to inflict on his government. Its impinging power was magnified beyond all reason, and so the resistance to it was made to assume the same awful nature. The ultimate victory of that which is good was not assured, in and of itself, and hence the desperate conflict with evil must be waged in every possible way. In morals as in medicine the heroic remedy has often arisen from a total misconception of the nature of the disease. A sin does not gain magnitude by being committed against God; the reverse rather. The conception of God is so remote from the mind transgressing as to occasion but a slight shock, the sin itself is so enclosed in God's patience, in his remedial processes, as to endanger nothing. It is an incident of the spiritual growth which he is pushing forward.

Its real measure and real mischief are found in its conscious presence and perverting power within the soul itself. We have to do with the man himself, rather than with the government of God existing beyond him and putting upon him crushing liabilities. Our liberty is of the largest order, a liberty to help the man in all ways to carry forward the living processes which inhere in his own thoughts.

The doctrine of sin sprang spontaneously from the crude efforts of the mind to awaken itself to its wide relations in a spiritual world, and it subserved a vital purpose in this connection. It marked a migration toward and into the unseen world. The theory of eternal punishment is fitted to subject minds, inert to spiritual motives, to urgent incentives, and to induce religious activity. It supplies by magnitude what it lacks in immediateness. It awakens attention and commands effort. It is a stringent appeal to moral quality. Insight, voluntary effort, play but a small part at any one time, in social renovation. A great accumulation of organic conditions, of historic forces, renders any immediate or considerable transformation impossible. Yet as personal action is that in which each man's power and responsibility centre, it becomes of the utmost moment to call out personal effort. No means are to be spared in doing this. The physician finds occasion to do all that in him lies to rally the energies of his patient, and to sustain the outer remedy by an inner impulse. The doctrine of future punishment is a sudden spasmodic effort to deepen spiritual sensibilities.

Voluntary activities, though comparatively insignificant at any one moment, assume chief importance when long periods are under consideration. If we were to compare the varieties, at any one time appearing in vegetable or animal life, with the great bulk of that life, they would seem very insignificant; yet these varieties are the determining features in reference to the future. They are pivotal points in the creative movement. Much the same importance in spiritual evolution attaches to any new activity in men's thoughts. Both in its coming and its going, in its formation and in its correction, in its excesses and in its defects, it serves to define the lines of progress and to renew its incentives.

Moreover, the terror of the terrific motive is greatly reduced by the dry, obdurate temper to which it is addressed. A few sensitive and exalted natures have been greatly harrowed and distressed by this excess of motive, but the great mass of men have had sensibilities suited to the goad. The lack of imagination, the inertness of a sensuous life, have left them at ease, as much at ease as the facts in the case could well tolerate. One may say that the magnitude of the motive was the direct product of the exigency. Men increased the sense of danger because no slight sense sufficed. The cruelty of the scourge was due to the callous quality of the skin. They substituted physical pain for spiritual failure because they understood the one and failed to conceive the other. We do not suppose this exaggeration to have been a conscious device of teachers, but instinctive in the minds of teachers and of taught alike. Men project their shadows in a gigantic and obscuring way on the path before them because the sun lies low behind them. Let it be in full strength overhead, and the shadows disappear.

These conceptions of future punishment alter their form as the need of them passes away. The unduly irritated sensibility serves at length to correct the doctrine by giving the conditions for a better understanding of the problem. When the mind comes to see that the chief penalties of ill-doing are enclosed in the ill-doing itself; that the ill-doing is ill-doing because of these inevitable evils it contains; that no extraneous physical inflictions can materially alter the evil facts but simply adds itself to them; when the mind grasps the problem of sin and evil in its own inherent terms as a spiritual and vital one, then these physical forms of punishment are felt to be irrelevant to it and disappear. When the sun is up, the clouds which have enveloped the earth and kept it warm are burned away. The spiritual transition must be made, but it must be made by a stage in growth, a sequence unfolding its reasons from within itself.

Chief among these dispelling powers is a better conception of the character of God, one less human and more divine, one bereft of passion and pervaded by love, one in which the gentle processes of growth take the place of an inflexible and barren formula of justice. The entire movement is evolutionary. First terms lead to later ones, and later ones arise in correction and enlargement of earlier ones. A distinct recognition of sin, even though it be accompanied by extravagant exaggeration, is an essential step in coming to a true knowledge of our relations to the spiritual world. In the criminal, we regard an aroused conscience, which makes the crime darken down the entire horizon, as a wholesome manifestation, and one which is likely to be followed by a more sober and just estimate of life.

In this direction have lain many theories of the atonement. A parent may be compelled to make a difficulty of forgiveness, lest a too ready relenting should lighten, in the mind of the child, the sense of the offence. The formal difficulty expresses to the uncultivated mind the actual difficulty. Forgiveness until seventy times seven is so high a law, one so purely spiritual, one that must be obeyed in so transcendent a temper, that it is inapplicable to a blind and sordid spirit. It must be climbed up to and then rejoiced in. The justiciary mechanism between man and God, which has characterized theological theories of the atonement, has delayed the approach of the sinner, and put upon him a sense of guilt and danger that has had regenerative power. It has been an essential step in disclosing the dividing nature of sin and its damaging results. The

Spiritual Phases of Evolution. 153

fundamental antagonism of sin and holiness must, in some way, lay hold of the mind, and if it is not laying hold of it on the spiritual side, it must do so on the legal, formal side. The true facility of forgiveness, its abiding facility, are hidden from the sinner as a sinner, and ought to be, so long as the mind is over-balanced to the side of transgression. It is only the spirit that is measurably cleansed of sin that can find a still further cleansing in the sweet sense of forgiveness. The blood of Christ cleanseth from all sin is an enforcement suited to one who in the darkness of an indolent and indifferent temper, or in a mood of mind full of temptation, would carry with him habitually unclean hands and an unclean heart. The successive theories of the atonement have been the spontaneous products of a definite spiritual culture, have wrought favorably on the minds of those to whom they have been addressed, and have finally given way before a deeper spiritual insight which they have helped to evoke. One climbs a mountain. Each succeeding step enables him to give a wider, more accurate, more stimulating construction to the landscape. The soul's later vision is a bird's eye view of what now lies beneath it. There is a sense in which drawing near to God is rising above the world, and reducing its obstructions and inequalities to their lowest terms.

The same considerations are applicable to the enforced authority of the Church, and to the enforced authority of the Scriptures. Man must be subject to authority. The assertion of authority is the assertion of law, and the assertion of law is the cardinal declaration of all worlds. The highest attainment is the inner discernment of the laws of life and the enforcement of these laws by the spirit on itself in glad liberty. But this is the end, not the beginning; the victory, not the struggle which precedes it. We must cover, in a painful experience, the period in which evil seems good and good seems evil; in which a pure and righteous law carries with it a sense of bondage—the period in which one is losing his life not winning it. This period of partial light and prevailing darkness is a long and checkered one in the growth of races. There are still few who habitually and profoundly feel that a life of pleasure, though ordered with utmost prudence, is immeasurably inferior to a life of service, though that service may be severe and often times unfruitful. The mind is not ready to cast itself unreservedly on God and the Kingdom of Heaven, and to find therein its inheritance of strength. A spiritually subjugated world is still to us not so beautiful and enjoyable a world as one in which we submit ourselves, more or less, to wayward impulses. Transcendent things are yet veiled from us as by a mist that lies low about us. The universal welfare of the entire human household does not appeal as strongly to us as those many delightful things which we can gather about our own homes. We cannot project the blessing near us outward till it falls upon the whole earth.

This period of estrangement must have its own motives. In it the spirit is not a sufficient authority unto itself. Some more extraneous authority must be set up in connection with which the sense of law can be called out. The spiritual child must have its spiritual nurture. The church collectively, as in the Catholic system, may take upon itself this brooding office. An aggregate greatness, matured by a thousand processes of growth, corrected by an ever enlarging experience, tempered by the goodness of many generations of good men, comes to be represented in the Church. The Church is thus the mother of men. This concentration and expression of authority in the Church was as inevitable as it was desirable. Many minds, emancipated from it, return to it with an insatiable longing. In it the best and truest convictions take to themselves a working form. To the masses of men who have no sufficient hold on the truth, who cannot make it a controlling and comforting law, a fellowship of faith, infused with the life of those who are leaders among men, is the very best substitute. What is wanting on the intellectual side is more than made up on the emotional side. Our spiritual experience is enveloped in the universal experience, and we often times do well to submit ourselves, at many points, to that experience. If we set up a rational law in a too personal way, we wander off into obscure places and lose the immediate incentives of life. There is a spiritual safety in marching with the great army of men. The difficulty encounters us when we undertake to carry forward these conjoint symbols and maintain the vitality of these common rites. A great organization becomes inert in the measure of its magnitude,

Spiritual Phases of Evolution. 157

and so what we gain in diffusion we lose in progress.

It was this fact which occasioned and justified Protestantism. Protestantism was the breaking away of vigorous minds from the bondage of belief—an effort to renew the march of ideas. As the authority of the Church was denied by it, and as men were still far from finding sufficient authority and unity by each one's hold on the truth, the Scriptures were assigned a central and controlling position. But the Scriptures remain a dead letter unless they, in turn, are enforced by each man's conscience, or gain a new interpretation and leadership in a church organization. Protestantism made for liberty of thought in the most active minds, but these, in preaching the Gospel as they conceived it, found occasion to fall back on the old method of a creed, an embodied discipline, as the suitable training of the people.

The Puritans are reproached for being so slow in seeing and accepting the doctrine of religious liberty. We forget that the view backward in religious faith is not the same as the view forward; that the discovery of truth and the enforcement of truth carry with them a difference of method. The spirit, in its movement forward, must claim and defend the right of search. When it comes, in turn, to propagate its beliefs, it naturally asserts their authority, and puts limitations on liberty. Those who are sluggish or dull or timid must be provided with stimulus and light and shelter. The free, bold mind has one law, the trammelled, dependent mind another law. Leadership is supplemented by a desire for guidance. Religious liberty is applicable only to religious life. It is a suitable and enjoyable prerogative only in connection with powers that demand it and can use it.

It is not strange then that men are slower in conceding than in claiming religious liberty. They claim it in behalf of the instinctive energy of a few minds; they withhold it in behalf of the disciplinary methods applicable to the mass of men. When liberty is weakness, it is not well to be free. When it is the loss of powers and not the use of powers, it becomes the disintegration, not the integration, of life. Protestantism by virtue of its liberty, has suffered reproach on this side as well as on the other. It has been looked upon as an insufferable dissolving away of religious ties;

a breaking up of the Catholic Church into innumerable and contemptible sects. While we must yield something to individual enterprise in exploiting the truth, we must also yield something to organic force in propagating it.

Much has to be learned at this point. Many are disturbed at the divisions among Christians. They are anxious to secure both unity and liberty. Liberty has destroyed unity. How shall that unity be restored? Certainly not by a sharp return to the stage of discipline; by reestablishing a creed and a ritual the same for all. This is to look backward not forward. This is to provoke a second time the attacks of liberty. The only unity that is possible to us is a growing unity of temper, a unity that converts discipline into a wider, unrestrained yet restrained, search for truth and for righteousness. That narrow discipline which is the nurture of immature powers is necessarily transitional and transient. The singleness of purpose, the Kingdom of Heaven, must confer unity and bring suitable guidance and constraint to the uses of truth. We cannot win unity by narrowing down belief into the skeleton of a creed, but by widening it out, till its essential and unessential centres, its more permanent and more variable parts, become plain to us. Truth is ultimately instrumental in the processes of life. Wide spiritual, social life will at once draw it into its own currents and correct it.

Authority, like government in the household, can only be transferred slowly from without inward. We are right when we do not in any way check this transfer; when we maintain authority, external if it must be, internal if it may be. Religious evolution is issuing in a slow uncovering of the true seats of authority in the soul itself, and in bringing forward this government with such insight and such submission as to make it adequate in the individual life, and sufficient for the ends of organization in the collective life. A collective life whose freedom takes nothing from its force, and whose force has ceased to be a burden on its freedom, is the goal towards which we are pushing. As the great mass of men are still in a stage of nurture, liberty, for the most part, lies beyond them. It is something they are to be aided in winning, rather than something to be laid at their feet. We suffer the confusion of conflicting interests incident to different

Spiritual Phases of Evolution. 161

powers. Our camp is like the camp of Jacob, which could not be hurried in its march because the children were tender and the flocks and the herds with young. The assertion of authority and the casting off of authority have alike been vital processes in the church. They have taken form under experience and under the pressure of special exigencies. We cannot expect very much to alter this movement. We can expect to make it, in different degrees, rapid, useful, and instructive. We guide our boat down the river; there is much in guidance, though the direction, the safety and the danger of our course are determined for us. Men slowly come into the light, and the light gives new conditions of activity. The inspiration of the Bible is a substitute for the insight of the Church, and both for the Spirit of Truth within the soul itself.

Perhaps no doctrine in the Christian creed has called out more ingenious and purely speculative thought than that of the Trinity. No doctrine more completely transcends our data than this doctrine. What is the significance of this protracted, and often times bitter, discussion, looked on as one term in the evolution of spiritual life among men? While our interpretation may fall sensibly short of the mark, it is plain that these discussions have not been as superfluous and unprofitable as many are inclined to regard them. They constitute a very important part of the means by which the mystery and greatness of the spiritual world and of the being of God have been impressed upon the minds of men. The provoking cause of the doctrine of the Trinity would seem to have been the doctrine of the divinity of Christ. The very obvious limitations which the incarnation brought with it, rendered it very difficult to include, in the personality of Christ, the entire life of God. There was a demand for a Godhead more comprehensive, more transcendental, than this assertion would imply. There must be some other adjustment of the divinity of Christ with the being of God. In removal of this difficulty, and of the further difficulty of the personality of the Holy Spirit, there sprang up the doctrine of the Trinity.

If we turn to the germ of the movement, the divinity of Christ, that doctrine is evidently the product of an effort to magnify and enforce and render determinate the revelation in Christ. Looked at spiritually, Christ is the way, the truth, and the life, by being the truth.

The truth is the connecting and the germinal term. Every one that is of the truth heareth my voice. It is not easy to understand how Christ can be anything to us aside from the truth, or beyond the truth. The truth is the one door between us and spiritual things. It is by that door we enter in. The difficulty with an unspiritual nature lies in the door. It does not swing easily or widely open to let the light into the spirit or the spirit into the light. The spiritual force of the world is hidden from the mind. It walks in the shadow of a great unpierced wall. Christ became a revelation by becoming a wide doorway of spiritual truth. The mind, still slow of perception and with a vision of short range, instead of looking through Christ into the Kingdom of Heaven looks at him, makes of him a mystery and begins to busy itself with his divine nature. The attention is thus diverted from a glorious revelation to an insolvable and a relatively unfruitful speculation.

The possibility of the dogma of the Divinity of Christ arises from the undue separation which men have made in thought between the world and God, and from the ease with which they lay aside physical facts as not truly expressive of the forces which lie back of them. A mystery in things—as in the doctrine of trans-substantiation—is thus made better than inner light. The sound of the word is more than its meaning; the image than the truth it reflects. It is not easy to understand how the personality of Christ should differ in its physical elements or in its intellectual constitution from the personality of man; nor how, if it did differ, we should be able to define the difference, his personality offering itself as it does under a strictly human guise; nor how any such difference could be of any great moment to us. We are saved not by what Christ is in the recesses of his own nature, but by the revelation of truth he makes to us under physical and intellectual facts and symbols familiar to us.

We are all the sons of God, children of his hand, our lives are a mystery to us. We are certainly in no condition to define our own physical dependence on God and the physical dependence of Christ, our own structure and his structure, and point out the differences between them. We have put upon ourselves a problem too hard for us, and one which God has not put upon us. Moreover, we are losing sight

Spiritual Phases of Evolution. 165

of the truthfulness and directness of God's methods. He does not deal in illusions. He does not offer us riddles and oracles which must first be untangled within themselves and afterward made serviceable. The physical facts of the world are his eternal speech, and full of his veracity. To make them other than they seem to be, to look upon them as disguises and then to strive to strip off the mask, is at once a disregard of the integrity of the world, and a greatly exaggerated estimate of our own penetrative and explanatory powers. We cannot thus make God's message to our minds and hearts a sober, coherent and instructive one. We are constantly diverting our attention from the thing signified to something in the manner of the delivery. It would seem as if all must admit that this question of the Divinity of Christ is to one side of the direct force of his words, and turns on a special rendering of special terms. We do not let the words lie in the very stream of the thought, but strive to make them separate sources of revelation.

When one like Christ stands before us in the flesh, goes in and out among us, talks with us, we are wise in accepting the sensuous character of the facts for what they seem to be, and in directing our attention in the channel of his thoughts, of his instruction. If we do not, we are at once in dreamland. We may regard him as a mere "docetism"; or as an embodiment of a divine being; or as some intermediate form of mystery. In any case, we are off the basis of verifiable facts, and beyond the region of inculcation. We are like the people of Lycaonia, who, in the presence of Paul and Barnabas, said: The gods are come down to us in the likeness of men. They first worshipped them and then stoned them. The facts before us do not respond with any decision to the theory we have put upon them, hence that theory shifts itself endlessly, is incapable of correction, and becomes more and more unfruitful. We can turn the doctrine of trans-substantiation into many forms, face with it for a thousand years the facts before us, and get nothing out of it which might not be much better gotten by a purely spiritual rendering of the sacrament.

If Christ is to offer himself to us with divine elements these must be found where, in the first instance, we failed sufficiently to find them—in his words. We may bewilder ourselves as much as we please about the make-up of his personality, about the exact character of its constituents and its genetic source, we still have no experience on these subjects. The more intelligent we become, the more perplexing and uninstructive is the assertion that Christ, as we know him, is the Second Person in the Trinity. Our conception of Deity refuses more and more to take on such limitations. Christ is the most to us when he is a way into the truth, and by the truth into life. As an open door he floods the world with light.

Does it follow from this that the doctrine of the Divinity of Christ has played no profitable part in the evolution of faith? Not in the least. We make stepping stones of our dead selves. What we fail to find adequately at one point, we are led to search for at another. Each lesser finding leads to the larger. Our religious conceptions become too comprehensive for any of the expressions we put upon them. All our experiences are symbols which imply a great deal and actually contain very little. They must all yield, like the glittering bubble, to the warm expansive breath that is in them; and when they cease to yield they will soon burst. There must be a constant shifting of symbols, because all of them are not equally adequate and none of them wholly adequate. The defects of each symbol become obvious and painful to us as our minds expand. We search for some fresh suggestion. It is of the nature of clouds, that float in the heavens and make their spaces real to us, to come and go and glide into each other in many ways. They are the parable of the spiritual terms of our being. These, too, must submit themselves to every change of temperature, every wind of thought. The fetich, the idol, the temple, the picture, the doctrine have all had symbolic force, have all been terms in development, and all exhaust their power. They are pernicious only when they refuse to give way. When men were laboring at the doctrine of the Father, the Son, and the Holy Ghost, they were at work under the law of their religious life; they were struggling with the overwhelming sense of mystery. When they cast aside these symbols and take in their place something less definite, they are equally under this law. The spiritual imagination weaves together our sensuous and super-sensuous life, and it does its work well when it never leaves our spiritual heavens vacant,—unless it be for a brief period in which the light and heat sweep away every image as an obstruction—and never for long occupies them with one set of symbols. We may climb up to God by virtue of priest, bishop, archbishop, pope. Having reached him, these intermediates utterly sink away.

The doctrine of the Divinity of Christ and of the Trinity have stood for the hold of men on the highest mystery. They have subserved a weighty symbolic purpose. Their very incomprehensibility has kept them fluent and serviceable. They have marked an inevitable and instructive transition in thought. These doctrines are much to be preferred to real, to blank, agnosticism. We say real, blank agnosticism, for it is almost impossible to keep agnosticism blank for any considerable period of time. It soon gathers its own meaning, takes on its own expression of the "unknown," and a mystery of ultimate being is put back of its words. Its disciples, like Spencer and Harrison, fall by the ears as to the nature of this spirit that begins to stir in the darkness beyond. The believing mind feels, in the very boldness of its faith, that it is dealing with the undefinable, and that its safety lies in that fact. "The assertion that Christ can not be very God of very God, in a sense infinitely beyond what may be truthfully said of all other human beings, is sheer intellectual presumption, is indeed dogmatism of the worst kind."* The mind of the writer thus relieved itself of the necessity of definition, because the negation was so undefinable and impossible.

One of the great reasons why this super-sensuous and unverifiable doctrine of the Trinity has had such a hold on the minds of men is that it remains the best symbol of mystery, most fully floods the spirit with the sense of mystery without altogether sweeping it from its footing. From time to time men put upon it some new terms of intelligibility, restore its symbolical power by associating the persons of the Trinity with some triple relation in the world about us—as the substantial phase, the personal phase, the truth phase of being. The very best and the very purest minds, men like Pascal, have had their thoughts deepened and their spiritual experiences enlarged by dogmas of this order. They have been vital whether we find them so or not.

* *The Christ of To-day.* p. 114.

The objections to these symbols are the objections to all symbols, the limitations, the embarrassments, they ultimately put upon the thoughts, the certainty with which they come to be regarded as exact and final statements of truth. From the moment they become fixed, they become oppressive. The incongruities they involve rise more and more to the surface. The mind is as active in casting them off as it was in constructing them. Our formulæ no longer reflect, like quiet waters, the deep heavens that stretch over them. We fall into a weary and restless state, and need again the refreshment of an active spiritual imagination.

If these doctrines are repeatedly softened, or ultimately displaced, by a deeper sense of the exclusively spiritual force of things, the movement lies wholly in the line of evolution. We learn to abide with God in his own changeable, daily revelation. We turn the world, by virtue of the life of the spirit, into thoughts, experiences, feelings, at one with the highest purposes of being. We need no remote speculation, no deep-sea dredging, for obscure nondescript forms. We are fully immersed in the lessons of life, which at once lie near us and stretch infinitely beyond us. The unchangeable term in this discipline is that it brings us nearer and nearer to God as pure Spirit. God is a spirit, and must be worshipped in spirit and in truth. We steadily shake off sensuous terms,—the sandals on our feet—and leave the too familiar symbol behind us that God may draw near to us and we to him, not in one way, but in all ways. Christ told his disciples, It is expedient for you that I go away, for if I go not away, the Comforter will not come unto you. The sensible presence must give way to the super-sensible, the more universal, presence, and thus the life of the disciple be more perfectly wrapped in the life of God. The spirit can neither pause nor turn backward in its search for the invisible; it has simply to learn to abide in it and with it as its own proper life. We are not to be subjected to any one presentation, any one method of thinking. If we are, it at length becomes barren to us. The spiritual world must lie near to us and far off, as the atmosphere to the bird, open in all ways of flight and in all directions.

This raises the question, can the mind accept growth as an ultimate result? Can it be found forever in new ways opposing the spirit to the letter, the large and impalpable to the narrow and palpable? Can it forever be breaking away from itself and yet thereby restoring itself more perfectly to itself? The secret of evolution is here. Each single step we take, we understand and magnify. Yet the steps beyond seem hazardous and fanciful. Virtue behind us reflects the light with unfailing brilliancy; virtue before us has not yet fully caught the light. It is because a vision of this high order comes and goes in the mind and can never be lost that the doctrine of spiritual life, spiritual evolution, becomes at once ideal and actual; something that we can no more escape than we can attain. We always lie under the creative hand at the centre of creative forces.

PART IV.

EVOLUTION IN THE PROOF IT OFFERS TO SPIRITUAL BELIEFS.

No! love which, on earth, amid all the shows of it,
Has ever been seen the sole god of life in it,
The love, ever growing there, spite of the strife in it,
Shall arise, made perfect, from death's repose of it!
And I shall behold Thee, face to face,
O God, and in Thy light retrace
How in all I loved here, still wast Thou!
Whom pressing to, then, as I fain would now,
I shall find as able to satiate
The love, Thy gift, as my spirit's wonder
Thou art able to quicken and sublimate,
With this sky of Thine, that I now walk under,
And glory in Thee for, as I gaze
Thus, thus! Oh, let men keep their ways
Of seeking Thee in a narrow shrine—
Be this my way! And this is mine!
Christmas-eve.
ROBERT BROWNING.

PART IV.

EVOLUTION IN THE PROOF IT OFFERS TO SPIRITUAL BELIEFS.

WE have now reached that which is most interesting in the doctrine of evolution, the confirmation it brings to our spiritual convictions. What evidence have we of the validity of our higher conceptions, their hold upon reality? Incomparably more than when they are left to rest, in a detached way, on certain supernatural phenomena, and are regarded as in a more or less violent manner in contention with the facts of the world. This conception strains faith to the utmost. If the world and the flesh and the devil are at war with righteousness, once for all, then, we must look to convulsive overthrow for its establishment—to some millennial transition, waited for so long in vain, still hidden so thoroughly out of sight in the events about us. This puts the mind, enveloped in the present darkness,—a darkness it exaggerates by coming out of the glare of revelation, —to the utmost stretch of belief, a belief that must lift it quite away from the forces everywhere pressing in upon it, rather than leave it in hopeful contact and concurrence with them.

Evolution, as a recent product of inquiry, easily takes on a bewildering glamour and is readily applied in a superficial and irritating way to earlier beliefs. Yet all knowledge from the beginning has prepared the way for it. All knowledge brings it immediate or remote confirmation. Evolution stands for the universality and continuity of intelligible relations, of creative processes. It takes its position as an assured theory, when the coherence of events has been established at a sufficient number of points to cover the general field of inquiry. The doctrine is closely associated with Darwin, because his researches in Biology removed the most familiar, and the most formidable, obstacle to its acceptance. We now claim, with a rush of thought the coherent, genetic force of events which so many things had suggested, but not established. Our present labor lies in that soberness of application which makes of evolution a key of knowledge.

This idea—which to the theist is nothing more than a sense of the thoroughness of God's thought—received into the spiritual world, makes it the final product, the adequate completion of the inorganic and the organic worlds. As the inorganic world has, in its unfolding, prepared the way for the organic world, so the two, in turn, lead up to and into the spiritual world. Man, on the physical side, the highest product of animal life, becomes also the first term in spiritual life, and, through the medium of society, grows into thoughts and feelings and activities that widen out into a Kingdom of Heaven. The sensuous takes on a super-sensuous force, and the super-sensuous, as in all fine art, gains an adequate sensuous rendering. Man comes increasingly under a law of beauty, a law of truth, a law of righteousness, and, with fitting and thoroughly sustaining impulses, builds up in purified society a spiritual product which we have long dreamed of as the Kingdom of Heaven. Under this conception strife passes by, all things become one and work with each other for their common fruition. The glory of this consummation has been with us as a faint morning twilight from the very beginning.

The earliest events, and subsequent ones increasingly, show a movement onward which is a revelation of order—the disclosure of a tranquil and brooding purpose. The universe is knit together by an eternal and under-girding thought. This conception is the most adequate and sublime possible, begins at once to get to itself the force of truth by its combining power, and lifts the mind to the point of utmost vision.

It alters our conception of the nature of truth. We are constantly speaking of the eternal and immutable character of truth. We do it in exaltation of the notion of truth. These adjectives are hardly applicable in the customary and narrow range of our knowledge. While truth stands primarily for physical facts, and the forces which are conceived as lying back of them,—the ever-flowing phenomena with which we are familiar—this affirmation of the eternity of truth is a figurative, rather than a literal, expression; stands for our confidence that we are in a world of significant, not meaningless, changes. The eternity of truth, however, is an affirmation too broad for these facts. The universe on its physical side, is a mobile product. It is continually passing

Evolution and Spiritual Beliefs. 183

away as well as continually becoming. The facts of to-day are not those of yesterday; much less is the knowledge of the present that of the past. The universe does not tarry in its nest. It is ever becoming another and superior product. Its laws, so called, take on new applications, assume new breadth. They multiply from below upward, as the range of vital, intellectual, and spiritual phenomena is increased. The universe does not submit itself to the statical idea which clings to the words eternal and eternal truth. God is known to us rather as a growing revelation than as a fixed formula or a perfected presence. We are compelled to conceive of facts as being constantly taken up into higher and more comprehensive ones; truth as leading to wider and more ruling ideas, and all things as returning into themselves by an upward movement before the notion of eternal truth gets for us the continuity and inexhaustible character of an intellectual product.

This fluent nature of truth is yet more apparent when we turn to its more appropriate meaning, the correspondence of the mind's conceptions with the underlying conceptions which bind the facts together. We then add more distinctly to the changeability of the facts the changeability of our thoughts concerning them. Truth becomes the super-sensuous term which lies between us and the universe about us, between us and the Divine Mind. It is the intellectual impression which that universe is fitted to make upon us, it is our rendering of it into thoughts, our approach to the Ruling Idea. Under this conception of truth, absoluteness and eternity are quite foreign to it. Truth, our truth,—and we know no other—is never complete, never absolute. It is always transitional, always pushing by growth into a more adequate expression. The mind moves in the rear of facts. Its activities lie in the direction of more ample knowledge, more perfect statement. The only thing in any way absolute is that we follow on to know the Lord.

It has been, especially in connection with religious inquiry, a very misleading conception, this absoluteness and eternity of truth. To affirm the eternity of the truth in the only form in which we have to do with it, to wit, our conceptions of things transcendental and moving forward in a transcendental way, is to destroy the truth as a vital power, is to bury beyond resurrection the intellectual germs planted in the mind.

We must, then, to begin with, under this notion of evolution, accept the truth as giving us directions of thought, axes of growth and no final product whatever. It is only the most abstract and formal statements, like those of mathematics, which are adequate and ultimate. The kernel of knowledge which we enclose in them has very little of this absolute character. There is relative firmness in physical elements, but when we come to study the forms they are taking on, the purposes they subserve, and the uses to which they can be put,—which alone define them—our exact statements are lost to us.

When we reach up to spiritual facts, we are dealing with truths as volatile as the germinating forces awakened in living cells. We can no more define, once for all, the paths we pursue, than birds can map out their lines of flight in the air. This is not feebleness in our lives, it is fulness; it is not the narrowness but the largeness of our powers. It is not the incomprehensibility of the things with which we are dealing, but their over-comprehensibility. We cannot, and we must not, in dealing with the validity of our spiritual conceptions under this notion of evolution, weigh them as final and sufficient formulæ of truth, but as suggestions of that which lies beyond, as transitional terms in spiritual growth.

The very magnitude of the conceptions with which we are dealing greatly reduces the danger of essential error. All our knowledge is gathered up by them, put on terms of dependence and made to partake in one common movement. If we study biological development at a single point, we may easily be confused. The wider the field the more certain the results. The unity and unfolding force of the divine thought secure, in the history of the world, a visible and undeniable expression. Its constituents, its cardinal events, the sweep of the movement, are all before us. The interspaces of confusion and disorder sink out of sight, are but the incidents of the pervading purpose. This conception of evolution is of the most comprehensive order. It embraces the physical world, the intellectual relations which these sensuous terms set in order, and the entire spiritual life interwoven with them and resting back upon them. Nor do we lose the sense of infinity which presses so close

Evolution and Spiritual Beliefs.

upon all our thinking. Though the upheavals of the divine thought nearest us, gaining form and light before us, fill and exhaust our vision, we are still left with our horizon—a circle of stellar worlds whose history lies far beyond us. Though the mountains on which we stand are of such magnitude, they have their setting in a universe commensurate with them. We are left, as it were, to one reverberating voice of truth that dies out in the remote distance and suffers no contradiction.

As this idea of evolution runs entirely through the world, its general anticipations and conclusions gain a correspondingly certain character. We cannot well be mistaken in them. There may be error at this point, or at that, but all things confirm the general result. Afloat on a river that feels in its tortuous windings each local cause, we may readily be confused as to its immediate bearings, but as to its general direction there can be no mistake. Forces of the most far-reaching and imperious order carry it forward. With the same clearness with which we see that physical life is ripening into intellectual life and intellectual life into social and spiritual life, that all things press upward into a purer, more divine presence, that there is and there can be no other trend in this comprehensive movement, that all conflicting tendencies are partial and temporary, mere eddies in the stream, a retreat simply to gain fresh vantage for progress, do we see that the one masterful current is cumulative, irresistible, and that we can trust ourselves to it with a certainty that knows no doubt.

Our theistic faith becomes comprehensive and sure; the most comprehensive, and so the most sure, of all the things the mind accepts. The character of God as it is revealed to us from within and from without, in the evolution of truth and in the evolution of its physical counterparts, is transformed into the most pregnant and prophetic term of the world. Prediction, hope, life, flow inevitably and freely out of it. We need no other assurance. The deeper we penetrate into the spirit of the world the more completely are we enveloped by it. This ruling idea, the character of God, is forever gaining disclosure in the universal movement. Scattered events, here and there, the mishaps which lie nearest to us, are capable of easy misapprehension, are already misapprehended by the hold they have on our feelings; but when we fall back on the ever-growing conception of God, and reason from it, light breaks in, not as from a lamp in one's hand, but as a diffused and increasing presence in the upper air, as lines of radiation from a centre not yet fully disclosed which lie quite athwart the clouds.

Take such a doctrine as that of everlasting punishment, the penalty of sin. It remains with men so long as they have not the ideas of justice, patience, renovation, grace which inevitably exclude it. As these ideas gain ground, this conception gives way. It ceases to have interpreting power. It becomes a perversion of the moral order, creative purpose and growing beauty of the world. It perishes from men's minds because the ideas which have nourished it are taking on higher forms. The irresistibleness of such a movement shows its divine authority, shows how deeply it is contained in the spiritual unfolding of our lives. A growing conception of the character of God is the fruition of all knowledge, and our new impulses under it have the force of a higher phase of life, the latest creative work of God. We can no more doubt this growing revelation of the world than we can distrust the dawn of day because many things still lie in shadow.

Our earlier impressions are rapidly giving way to clearer and more extended ones. The external support we can bring to any single dogma to which we may hang our faith, like the inspiration of Scripture, is slight indeed compared with this direct resting back on God in the entire creative process, in an evolution we are daily sharing. From this ruling conception all light flows, and the moment any belief begins to cast a baneful shadow nothing hinders our setting it aside. We are working with light and that only. This is the logic of our spiritual life, the coherence of the spiritual world on which we are entering. We fear nothing because the shadows are fleeing away. We share with the Samaritans a new sense of truth. Now we believe not because of thy saying, for we have heard him ourselves and know that this is indeed the Christ, the Savior of the world.

It is by virtue of this relatively independent and growing hold of each mind on the truth that we reconcile instruction and insight, submission and mastery. We can be led by Christ into the truth, but being there we are no longer led. Many may help us in forming our conceptions of God, but that conception,

Evolution and Spiritual Beliefs.   191

being formed, rules the mind by its own power. The doctrine of evolution discloses to us the divine mind with the largest possible accumulation of details and with the most overwhelming force. Hence prophetic vision, faith, the light that lies athwart the future gathers at once assurance. We have found God and are at rest.

We urge this growth of belief in one more direction. We have framed an induction under the doctrine of evolution of the most comprehensive character, and so we are entitled to its conclusions and its consolations. We remind ourselves again of what we have to show, of what is involved in a spiritual evolution of the race. Earlier conceptions are not to be regarded as simply misleading illusions, but as germinating ideas. An idol is a primitive rendering of a spiritual presence. It is serviceable until its inadequacy and its incompatible elements come to be felt. Later conceptions, as that of God immanent in the world, are the product of the same tendency under growing knowledge. They are authoritive in the measure of the wider survey that lies back of them. The nature of this growth in the conception of God may be hidden from us by the fact that it is less and less capable of accepting a final formula, is more and more a product of the spiritual imagination. The corrective process by which the notion of the Absolute gains its true dimensions is one by which we cast aside limitations rather than set them up. We are not, for this reason, to regard it as a negative result. We are not being pushed farther and farther into the unknown.

In philosophy and in religion, scepticism, of a negative character, has always proved weak. Not till some positive enlargement of truth has been offered do inadequate notions begin to give way. There is no discipleship of negations. The chief service of scepticism is to compel a reformation of ruling ideas. The corrected conception is more pervasive and controlling than the earlier one. Thus the notion of a Divine Presence becomes a supreme factor in spiritual life, and spiritual life takes to itself all forms of life. With this assertion before us of an ever-expanding spiritual experience in the race, a more systematic, comprehensive, and general grasp of the truth, we turn to the inductive argument.

Our intellectual experiences involve three elements, an instinctive, a rational, and an ethical one. Each of these implies an increas-

Evolution and Spiritual Beliefs. 193

ing hold of our spiritual life on the facts which surround it and nourish it. Instincts stand for the unconscious responses of animal life to its circumstances. They are very general and subtile methods of adjustment, which prepare the way for later development. Instincts, as primary adaptations, may be outgrown and may give place to higher methods. It does not belong to them, however, to be widely or for any considerable period, out of relation to the physical world. The animal is not possessed of one tendency while his circumstances call for another. Corrections set in and the instinct regains its footing. Any other result would leave the world and the life it nourishes out of harmony. It is a matter of surprise when any of these organic tendencies are, even in a narrow way, unserviceable.

A belief in spiritual beings and influences has something of the spontaneous and universal force of an instinct. In its earlier forms especially it is inevitable, blind, controlling. We are bound to believe, under the notion of evolution, that this irrepressible and widely influential recognition of super-sensuous forces stands for a correspondingly weighty fact; that it indicates a new adjustment, in its earlier stages, of seen to unseen things, and may easily be a first term in an entirely fresh form of development. We are certainly not at liberty to think of it as a surreptitious impulse, confusing the lines of progress. The coherence and universality of causes do not admit of such a supposition. The moment we discover an instinct in animal life, we are put on an inquiry into its relations, knowing that these will be valid and important. The instant we recognize the universal movement of men toward a spiritual, as opposed to a sensuous world, we must be prepared to see in it the introduction to a new and higher experience. If we do not, we fall off from the doctrine of evolution, we lose the clue to coming events.

So far as our spiritual conceptions are rational,—and they are growingly rational—this sense of adaptation and reliability is increased. None of us is so far prepared to invalidate reason as to disparage this growth of the more consistent, out of the less consistent, conception. We have no other instrument with which to weaken its force than reason itself. We are disposed rather to accept the more blind, instinctive belief for the sake of the more rational one to which it gives rise. We find a

Evolution and Spiritual Beliefs.

double inductive argument, first in the darker, second in the clearer relation, both lying in the line of evolution. So far as our growing spiritual conceptions are the product of reason, they must be increasingly adjusted to the world in which we are, and to our own inner life in its mastery of it. To think otherwise is to discard reason, break down the processes of thought, and fall back into utter confusion. We cannot sustain reason for ends of unbelief without also fully sustaining it for the ends of belief. It is involved in religion, it is involved in philosophy, it is involved in science, that the processes of thought are essentially sound; most pertinent to the events which enclose us; open to correction, and capable of correction in the lines of movement which they themselves lay down. Any diving deeper than this brings up nothing but dirt. There is thus an induction as nearly universal as any induction can be, since it grows out of our entire experience and gains force with it, that our rational processes in their inherent and inevitable tendencies, are the most deep-seated possible adjustments to the real world which envelops us. It is simply an application of the universal principle that every effect has some adequate cause, that the world visible and invisible, is knit together in perpetual action and reaction. On this increasing continuity and coherence of reason, rests the order of the spiritual world. It stands in the upper realm for precisely that which causation stands for in the lower realm. So far, therefore, as a rational tendency gains footing in an instinctive one, and leads to a spiritual experience, it widens the world in which we are, and lies in the line of the fullest expression of its forces. It is at one with the integrity of the entire movement.

The ethical element raises this presumption of validity to its highest terms. Ethical ideas develop in connection with spiritual ones, in a social experience increasingly permeated by the laws of conduct. The phenomena and the laws suited to them come together. As in the two tables, four commands turn on spiritual and six on social relations, so has it ever been. A better conception of God means better morality, and better morality a better conception of God. But none of our powers lay hold on truth with more conviction and authority than do our moral powers. The law gains strength as it gains breadth and clearness. It is impossible to think of an ethical development along a line of increasing unreality. Ethical growth, more than any other, means an insight into facts, and an increasingly accurate adjustment to them. The gain, therefore, of "social tissue" in ethical rightfulness, which has accompanied the expansion of religious conception,—such as is shown in the first and second great command—declares, with an invincible inductive force the integrity, the validity, of the process of which it is a part. Our spiritual life cannot have grown by fastening on unreal and vanishing ideas. It stands, and has ever stood, for our closest contact with realities. We may rest, therefore, assured with that assurance which is the aggregate force of knowledge, that the general movement of our spiritual life is into the light and under the deepest forces which touch the world. We are dealing with realities which evade us only because they are so subtile and comprehensive. We cannot grasp the air with the hand, but if we are content to breathe it it carries vitality to every portion of the body. The noblest and the best of men have thriven, and pre-eminently thriven, by means of spiritual conceptions which had lost for them their illusory character.

The hold which the mind gains on the world by virtue of spiritual conceptions is especially seen in the prophetic temper. Forecast is inseparable from knowledge. We no sooner see the evolutionary laws of the world than we discover whither they are tending. It is inevitable that every period, deep and devout in its spiritual life, should entertain a Messianic conception; should feel the stir in the soil of faith's germs; should anticipate a coming Spring as the forces of the Kingdom of Heaven disclose themselves. The knowledge of the Lord shall cover the earth as the waters cover the sea. So every spirit feels in whom the revelation of divine things is entering. The assertion only expresses its astonished sense of the latent power of spiritual truth.

Though our hopes about this or that event may not be any proof that the thing desired will occur, these hopes, when they stand for the inner impulse of growth present in the human soul, may be the most undeniable proof. They are, then, the forerunners of a life adequate for its own ends, and forcing its way upward. From this point of view, men have not attached too much importance to the prophetic temper. They have erred only

Evolution and Spiritual Beliefs. 199

when they regarded some narrow expression of it as more significant than the underlying impulse. None of us can anticipate the precise events of the opening season ; we can all predict the many and wide victories of awakened life. Definiteness of Messianic prediction is a groping of the mind in darkness ; the prophecy itself is the soul's certainty of spiritual things.

No doctrine so rests on this prophetic force of the spirit as that of immortality. Neglecting a few exceptions as of no practical moment, we may affirm that this belief has appeared, and is sure to appear, in the measure in which the higher ethical life is present. It is the inevitable forecast of the spirit when it is in any good measure awakened to its own powers. It is a truth that can hardly be told to a man,—if thou be the Christ, tell us plainly— it must be discovered by him, be found within himself as the inner force of his own life. My words they are spirit and they are life. It is wholly in this temper that Christ involves it in the facts which he is interpreting. The water that I shall give him shall be in him a well of water, springing up into everlasting life. Everlasting life is not so much something to be given as something already given, potential in the power of the spirit. Whosoever liveth and believeth in me shall never die. The mind once fully possessed of a sense of its own divine nature cannot doubt that all things will submit themselves to that nature. That events should make way before the spirit is no longer a marvel, is a fact of the same order as the bursting of the bud and the blossoming of the flower, the hourly miracle of life. Christ finds immortality in the soul of man, in its hold on truth. On the side of God, he finds it in the scope of his purposes. God is not the God of the dead but of the living. He robs himself of his own work if he allows Abraham, Isaac, Jacob, to sink into dust. There cease to be storehouses of divine wisdom. The ephemeral character of his creations would mean the ephemeral character of his own life. God cannot be the God of the dead. Myriads cannot constitute an animal kingdom, much less a Kingdom of Heaven. Immortality lies at the basis of the greatness and grandeur of the spiritual world. We first discover this world and then its implications. Ye believe in God, believe also in me, expresses the inner coherence of spiritual truth.

Nothing can take the place of this genetic force of ideas; nothing can withstand it. Belief in God carries all things with it. We live and move and have our being in him.

We often speak of a scientific sense. We frequently observe the want of it in men otherwise excellently endowed. It lies chiefly in a recognition of the significancy of a tendency inductively established, its ruling power in all directions. As the merest thread of nervous fibre is carefully traced, and its function sought for, so every indication of sequence is laid hold of by the scientific mind as an unmistakable clue to structure.

These is also a spiritual sense, a power to feel spiritual connections and to discover their implications. It is an inductive tendency exercised in a higher region. It has the constructive force of an artistic temper. It is as real as the most real thing, and as subtile as the most spiritual thing. It is in the doctrine of evolution that these lower and higher impressions find their ultimate harmony, parts of one expanding, intellectual whole.

It is this sense that pronounces on immortality. It is this sense, that once accepting immortality, gives no further room for doubt.

The idea becomes more and more the centre of all the mind's spiritual constructions. Without it events fall back into chaos. This growth of the doctrine by internal accretion rather than by external accumulation is wholly rational, and peculiarly rational in connection with evolution. The one grand movement on which the mind has fastened is that toward spiritual life. This movement cannot be stayed, cannot be restricted, any more on its spiritual than on its physical side. The two are henceforth inseparable. But spiritual life means nothing more than the increasing force which the mind itself is able to attach to super-sensuous convictions; as the scientific temper stands for its hold on physical relations. As forecast is the power to apprehend events still in the distance, so spirituality is the power to lay hold of ethical convictions and affections as the most adequate and effective terms in life. The ethical temper easily reaches the super-sensuous thought through the sensuous form; finds back of the near and the immediate the distant and the remote, and this along the lines of evolution. God is a being to be thought of less and less sensuously, to be rejoiced in more and more super-sensuously. The spiritual government of the world and its highest incentives are first found within the mind itself, and later meet with confirmation beyond it, a confirmation which is the replication of its own insight. Immortality is not to be proved sensuously; so proved it would lack its chief significance. It would lie in direct extension of physical things. It is to be proved super-sensuously, as the presence and power of those truths whose fitting expression it is. It must grow out of, and it must be grafted on, its own form of life. Immortality as a belief must be an achievement, the thrust of the mind itself towards life, if it is to have the power of a spiritual belief. It must go forth from the soul's own experience, and be taken hourly back into that experience. Otherwise it becomes an external dogma on which, in any moment of darkness, the mind loses hold. It will have the force of a lurid portent or the peaceful presence of a guiding light just in the measure in which the life declares it, and draws near to it, in its daily unfolding.

We reason wisely when we reason from that which is best in us. The best is best, because of its higher, wider adaptations. The better conception, the more comprehensive, harmonious idea, is like the stronger life, it is the thing that is to survive. The conception of immortality justifies itself as the conception which gives new power to spiritual life. It carries it to a higher plane, and there unfolds it. It marks a distinct stage in evolution.

The facts confirm this theoretical estimate of its force. The doctrine of immortality, as entertained by men, has ennobled them and given them greatly increased power. It has been an essential incentive in widening spiritual impulses and rendering them victorious. We may not, therefore, deny it a place in that development by which the forces of a spiritual world are brought together. Valid as an existing power, it is valid as a part enclosed in a larger whole.

The mind does wisely when it follows in the rear of ruling ideas. Our roads are well laid out when they accept the lead of the brooks. They thread the ravines and reach the fruitful plains associated all the way with the quiet murmur, bright reflection, and unstaying flow of a cosmic force.

It is certainly in keeping with the spiritual evolution which we are affirming, that its one essential term, immortality, arises in the mind itself as one of the earliest products of its new life. This is what spirituality means, the power of the spirit to envelop the sensuous world with a true heavens, the two in living interplay. This is that stage of creation with which we are all busy, the establishment of a firmament—which the Scriptures call Heaven—dividing the waters which are under it from the waters which are above it, and so making ready for a second day in the cosmic movement. The world moves; this is the very substance, the underlying condition, of knowledge. But whither does it so certainly and obviously move as toward a spiritual life ever renewed by invisible relations with God and with man? Here is a creation that compacts the world into one purpose and discloses the power of all that has been done, and all that remains to be done—a creation which is the embodied wisdom and love of God. When we discover evolution as the dynamic force of truth, the Spirit of Truth begins to disclose all things to us. The nidus of the world, physical and spiritual, lies before us.

THE END.

RECENT THEOLOGICAL WORKS

Gospel Criticism and Historical Christianity.— A Study of the Gospels and of the History of the Gospel-Canon during the Second Century; together with a Consideration of the Results of Modern Criticism. By ORELLO CONE, D.D. Second edition (uniform with the above), 8vo, gilt top, $1.75.

"The work of a scholar who has made himself familiar with the most important recent investigations, and who appreciates the nature and bearing of the questions at issue. . . . Replete with information for those who have not made the subject a specialty, and executed in a spirit of candor and rational inquiry."—GEO. B. STEVENS, Prof. of New Testament Criticism in Yale University, in *Yale Review*.

"A thoroughly scholarly work; its tone is deeply reverent and spiritual, and its literary style is marked by sobriety and conspicuous refinement and grace. . . . It has commanded throughout our close attention and frequent admiration."—*Literary World* (London).

The Gospel and Its Earliest Interpretations.— A Study of the Teaching of Jesus and its Doctrinal Transformations in the New Testament. By ORELLO CONE, D.D. Uniform with "Gospel Criticism." 8vo, gilt top, $1.75.

The object of this work is to elucidate the teaching of Jesus, and to present, both in their relation to it and to one another, the principal types of religious doctrine contained in the New Testament. The pursuit of this object has led to a consideration of the resemblances and differences which exist between the word of the Master and the interpretations of it by his followers, who composed the New Testament. The author's scholarship and candor, his clear conception of the development of religious thought in the New Testament, and his refined and forceful style render this one of the foremost books of the year in its department.

The Bible: Its Origin and Growth and its Place among the Sacred Books of the World. Together with a List of Books for Study and Reference. With Critical Comments. By JABEZ THOMAS SUNDERLAND, author of "What is the Bible?" 12mo, $1.50.

"To-day thinking people on every side are asking, and with an insistence and earnestness wholly unknown in the past, the question: What has an honest, independent, and competent biblical scholarship—a scholarship that investigates and speaks in the interest, not of theological dogmatism, but of truth—to tell us about the Bible, as to its origin, its authorship, its real character, its place among the great sacred books of the world, its permanent value?"—*Extract from Preface*.

RECENT THEOLOGICAL WORKS

The Church in the Roman Empire, A.D. 64-170.
—With Chapters of Later Christian History in Asia Minor. By Prof. W. M. RAMSAY, of the University of Aberdeen, author of "The Historical Geography of Asia Minor." 8vo, with maps, $3.00.

"It is a book of very exceptional value. Prof. Ramsay is a real scholar, and of the very best type of scholarship. A thoroughly good book; a product of first-hand and accurate scholarship; in the highest degree suggestive; and not only valuable in its results, but an admirable example of the true method of research."—*The Churchman.*

St. Paul the Traveller and the Roman Citizen.
By W. M. RAMSAY. With maps. One vol., 8vo, cloth, $3.00.

"A work which marks an important step in advance in the historical interpretation of St. Paul. . . . Professor Ramsay has made a solid and valuable contribution to the interpretation of the Apostolic literature and of the Apostolic age—a contribution distinguished no less by ripe scholarship, independent judgment, keen vision, and easy mastery of material, than by freshness of thought, boldness of combination, and striking originality of view."—*The* (English) *Speaker.*

Christian Theism: Its Claims and Sanctions.—
By D. B. PURINTON, LL.D., President of Denison University. Gilt top, 8vo, $1.75.

"President Purinton's work on 'Christian Theism' seems to me a remarkably good book, which may be strongly recommended to thoughtful readers, and is partially well suited to be a text-book for classes. It treats of various sides of the subject, with vigorous thought, clear arrangement, and in a style that is at once terse and lucid."—JOHN A. BROADUS, D.D., LL.D., President Southern Theological Seminary, Louisville, Ky.

Paganism Surviving in Christianity.—By ABRAM HERBERT LEWIS, D.D., author of "Biblical Teachings Concerning the Sabbath and the Sunday," etc. etc. Gilt top, 12mo, $1.75.

"The book is full of the enlightenment which an earnest student can throw upon a great religious and moral question. It is not sectarian or polemical. No one could call it heretical, for it shows how papanism was transmitted among the followers of Christ, and how tardily it has been fading away under the benign influence of Christian civilization."—*Phila. Eve. Bulletin.*

www.ingramcontent.com/pod-product-compliance
Lightning Source LLC
Chambersburg PA
CBHW031828230426
43669CB00009B/1268